TEXAS A&M

Where Have You Gone?

RUSTY BURSON

FOREWORD BY
EMORY BELLARD

WWW.SPORTSPUBLISHINGLLC.COM

Director of production: Susan M. Moyer
Acquisitions Editor: Mike Pearson
Developmental editor: Doug Hoepker
Project manager: Greg Hickman
Book design: Jennifer L. Polson
Dust jacket design and imaging: Kenneth J. O'Brien
Copy editor: Cynthia L. McNew
Photo editor: Erin Linden-Levy
Cover photo: Mark Jones

ISBN: 1-58261-753-8

Printed in the United States.

To Vannessa, my wife, my partner, my inspiration and my favorite companion for the countless Aggie sporting events we have attended through the years. To Payton and Kyleigh, my future Aggies and my pride and joy. And to my sister, Lindsey, one of the most passionate sports fans I know. One of these days, the spirit of Aggieland may just overcome you, too.

CONTENTS

AGGIE FOOTBALL GREATS

ADDITIONAL AGGIE GREATS: BASEBALL, BASKETBALL, TRACK, AND VOLLEYBALL

FOREWORD
BY EMORY BELLARD

It's been some three decades since that November day when the Texas Longhorns came calling at Kyle Field for one of the most anticipated games in the storied history of the traditional rivalry.

In 1975, our team scratched and clawed its way to a 9-0 record, led by a stifling defense and an efficient offense. The electricity leading up to the big game with the Longhorns was so incredible that I can still sense it to this day. Before a packed house at Kyle Field, I can still visualize Bubba Bean flashing down the field in that maroon striped jersey for a run that set up the game-sealing field goal.

The Aggies won that game, 20-10, and it's still one of the most memorable days of my life. We didn't quite pull off the ultimate goal of the national championship, as Arkansas beat us a week later. But no one can take away the feeling I had as I watched our players celebrate with the A&M fans inside Kyle Field.

This great game of college football really is about the young men, who at Texas A&M—more than anyplace else—have had a special bond with the 12th Man in the stands. Our players back in the 1970s—as they have been throughout the history of Aggie football—were part of a special family. And that kinship has continued long after the last long run or touchdown pass on the football field.

I think fondly upon guys like Tank Marshall, Mark Dennard and Phil Bennett, great college players who have gone on to be successful in their lives after their playing days concluded. I have also admired from afar the class of Kip Corrington, the fire of Dan Campbell, the strength of Reggie Brown and so many of the other athletes from all sports that appear in this book.

While A&M's last national title in football came in 1939, the distinguished list of football players and good people who have put on the maroon and white uniform is as impressive as that from any school with multiple national championships.

In the enjoyable chapters of this book, reading up on their successes as players and their accomplishments as businessmen and women, husbands and wives, and mothers and fathers really has rekindled a lot of great memories for me as I recall my time in Aggieland. Rusty Burson truly catches the personalities of the former players featured in the book, and each story reminds me of the important role that athletics can play in the lives of the individuals who participate.

You can tell that each of the players featured has applied the same determination and resolve they once used on the fields and courts at A&M to their personal and professional lives. As a former coach, nothing brings me greater satisfaction than seeing the young men I coached go on to succeed in their lives after they have played their final games. I'm sure most every other coach feels the same way. And that's why this "Where Have You Gone?" format was so appealing to me.

As for where I've gone, I'm still in Texas, living in Georgetown and playing golf as often as my wife allows. I still keep tabs on the Aggies, and I still look back on my time as the head coach at Texas A&M with tremendous appreciation for the men and women who helped make my time in Aggieland so special. There are so many reasons why Texas A&M is a special place, from the traditions to the spirit that has been fostered since the school first opened its doors. But people really make the place. And Aggies everywhere should be proud of their student-athletes over the years.

This entertaining, well researched and well written book re-emphasizes what a special place Texas A&M is, and what kind of wonderful student-athletes the school produces. Many things have changed at Texas A&M since I was last on the sidelines at Kyle Field, but the fabric for success has always been the people on campus. Fortunately, some things at Texas A&M never change.

PREFACE
BY RUSTY BURSON

I realize I'm not alone with the admission that I am in debt. According to the Nilsen report, the nation's 151.9 million credit cardholders owned an average of 9.1 cards with an average outstanding balance of $405 per card. That's an average of $3,685 per cardholder. And that's not even considering consolidation loans, car loans, mortgage loans, etc.

But even when you factor in all those things, I'm probably in a debt league of my own. Fortunately my credit history doesn't actually reflect this, but by my own estimation, I still owe about $3 million—$1 million apiece to the key contributors—as a result of the 1992 Texas A&M-Texas Tech game. In fact, I owe my life as I know it to former A&M athletes.

Thankfully, it's not a real debt and the would-be collectors—Jeff Granger, Greg Schorp and Terry Venetoulias—aren't holding their breath or beating down my door regarding the receipt of payment.

"Oh no," Venetoulias said with a laugh. "I gave up on my $1 million share a long time ago. After all, the requirement was that you had to make it big, bring in the big bucks. Rusty, have you played the lottery lately? Are you feeling lucky?"

Uh, no. But I am lucky in love thanks to Texas A&M's 19-17 victory over Texas Tech in 1992 on the game's final play. One of the Aggie fans in attendance that day was a beautiful brunette who had graduated from A&M the year before. She was living in Clear Lake at the time, but came to College Station for the game and to visit friends to leave some worries behind. Her intention was to return to Clear Lake immediately after the game.

But because of the fantastic nature of the finish, her friends convinced her to stay and celebrate the Aggies' win. At about that same time, my friends were convincing me to do the same. I was the sports editor of the *Galveston Daily News*, and I had come to College Station simply to cover the game. In fact, it was the first game *12th Man Magazine* editor Homer Jacobs, who at the time was working for another magazine that followed Aggie athletics, and I had ever covered together.

Jacobs and others didn't need to do much arm-twisting to convince me to stay. The thrill of the victory and the nature of the fantastic finish required a celebration. If the Aggies had lost, I would simply have gone home. If Granger had not escaped a sure sack late in the fourth quarter and found Schorp over the middle, that beautiful brunette from Clear Lake would have done the same. And if Venetoulias had missed the last-second field goal, neither she nor I would have wound up at the Dixie Chicken.

But all of those things happened perfectly, and after a masterful sales job on my part (along with some begging and pleading), that woman became the love of my life. We were married 10 months later, and as you might imagine, the "War Hymn" was definitely a focal point of our reception.

Winning may not be everything, but winning that particular game has certainly meant everything to me. Vannessa and I have been married since 1993, and we have two wonderful children. I literally owe Granger, Schorp and Venetoulias more than they can imagine. Of course, they'll have to imagine ever receiving any actual payments.

Ever since that day in 1992—and especially since my own life was so dramatically shaped by a football game—I have been fascinated by how Aggie athletics impacts the lives of so many for so long. And one of my favorite personal and professional pastimes is catching up with the A&M stars of yesteryear to see how their lives have been shaped by the time they spent on the fields, courts and classrooms of Texas A&M. The more stories I do of this nature, the more impressed I am by this place called Aggieland.

This book is a labor of love for me because it contains so many stories I love to tell. Antonio Armstrong and Reggie Brown are amazing young men who have stared adversity in the face and never flinched; Phil Bennett and Bill Schroeder are remarkable survivors; Joe Boyd and Tommy Maxwell possess two of the most incredible Christian testimonies I've ever heard; Stacy Sykora has more personality and energy than anyone I have ever encountered; Sirr Parker has overcome more in his lifetime than most of us can ever imagine. The list goes on and on. My only problem in writing this book was attempting to limit it to 40 subjects. Alas, I couldn't even do that, as 41 chapters appear within. I truly could have written 80 or more, and there are so many other wonderful men and women I wish I could have included.

Some of the names that appear in this book are as well known to Aggie fans as Gen. Earl Rudder or E. King Gill. Others are a little more obscure. But the resounding theme throughout this book is that every one of these former A&M athletes was touched, sharpened, enhanced and better prepared to face the daily battles of real life because of his time at Texas A&M. This is a special place that develops unique qualities and characteristics in the men and women who come to school in College Station.

I hope you enjoy reading these stories as much as I enjoyed compiling them. And I hope you are reminded—as I am every day by the company I keep in my own home—that the games and seasons end quickly, but the benefits of being a part of them can last a lifetime. I'm forever in debt to Aggie athletics. Not to mention MasterCard, Visa, and American Express.

ACKNOWLEDGMENTS

Thanks to the entire staff and donor base of the 12th Man Foundation. It's a pleasure to be associated with such a first-class organization, and I am grateful to all the donors for their support and constant feedback. The staff of the 12th Man Foundation includes some of the world's best people. But what else would you expect from a group that goes to work every day inside a football stadium? While the entire staff is terrific, I would like to extend a special thanks to Miles Marks, Homer Jacobs, Trey Wright and Reagan Chessher. You have all been so much more than bosses and coworkers. You are great friends, sounding boards and sports authorities. I appreciate your ideas, input, support and contributions to this book and *12th Man Magazine*.

I'd also like to thank all of the athletes who have been so willing to share their stories and time for this book and all the other "flashback" stories we have worked on together since *12th Man Magazine* started in 1996. Many of you have become friends, and many more of you have served as a tremendous example to me, my children and the entire Aggie family with your values, sacrifices, character, work ethic and more.

To Chuck Glenewinkel, Colin Killian, Debbie Darrah, Brad Marquardt, Steve Miller and the rest of the sports information staff at Texas A&M, I can't say thanks enough for all your help through the years. You are the best in the business, and I'd expect nothing less from a department headed by the classiest, most diligent, hardest-working and professional SID on the planet—Alan Cannon. I could use many of those same descriptions about Cathy Capps with the Lettermen's Association. Thanks, Cathy, for all the contacts, help and conversations I've enjoyed with you. And I'd also be remiss without thanking Hank Presler for his enthusiastic effort on this project and many others.

Finally—and foremost—I thank God for this opportunity. When I started in journalism, I vowed to myself and to the Lord that I would never minimize an athlete's faith in my stories. I'm not always very good at sharing my own testimony, but hopefully, I've helped some of the athletes I've been blessed to work with share theirs. I don't really think God cares who wins or loses a football, basketball or baseball game. But He is the ultimate source of victory, and I am most thankful to be on His team and to have come in contact with so many A&M athletes who are also playing for a much higher purpose than a conference or national title.

Where Have You Gone?

Aggie Football Greats

JOE BOYD

As Joe Boyd waited in the hospital for the doctor's diagnosis, he knew something was terribly wrong. Boyd was as tough as a $2 steak and possessed a mean streak as wide as the Brazos River. He boxed for fun, wrestled as a hobby and regularly went for blood like a shark on a feeding frenzy.

But on this particular day in 1938—following Texas A&M's season-ending victory over Rice—even Boyd's battle-tested pain tolerance was being pushed to the limit. The throbbing in his neck was so severe that Boyd wasn't the least bit surprised when doctors discovered cracked vertebrae. He also suffered broken ribs and endured temporary paralysis in his legs from the beating he took in the game, but it was his neck that was causing him the most torment.

"The man came out of the X-ray room and said my neck was broken," Boyd recalled from his home in West Union, W.V. "I said, 'I knew there was something wrong.' I was a tough old bird, but it absolutely bothered me."

It did not, however, prevent Boyd from playing the following season. In a testament to Boyd's toughness, he not only played the entire 1939 season, but he also was named to six All-America teams and, along with John Kimbrough, led the Aggies to the school's only national cham-

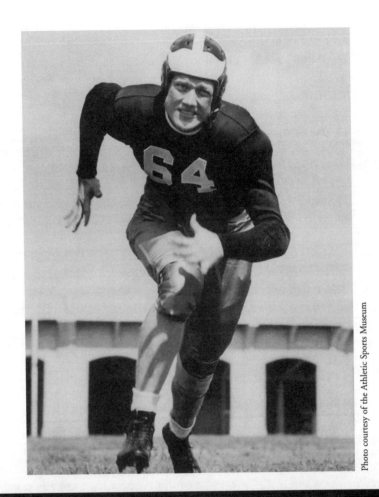

Photo courtesy of the Athletic Sports Museum

JOE BOYD
A&M Letterman: 1937-1939

Position: Offensive Lineman, Defensive Lineman
First-team All-SWC tackle: 1938, 39
All-American: 1939
Member of *Sports Illustrated*'s 25-year All-America team

pionship. Boyd was the anchor of an unyielding defense that allowed just 31 points over the entire season. With Boyd up front, the Aggies had fewer cracks in their defense than discovered in Boyd's own X-rays.

"They hired a big, strong woman to massage my neck between games in 1939 and absorb the chips that came off that break," said Boyd, who turned 86 in 2003. "Then I would go back in and play on Saturdays with a cracked neck. It caused me plenty of pain, but I was just happy to be at A&M considering my background."

Boyd's background was as hard as his backbone. He was born in Jacksonville, Texas, but soon afterward, his family moved to Dallas, where Boyd's tough-guy image began to take shape. By the time he was a teenager, Boyd was a member of one of the numerous gangs in the Dallas area during the early 1930s.

The city's answer to the gang problem was to organize the members into sports teams—the West Dallas gang, the Fair Park gang and so forth. Each of the gangs fielded a football team, and it was there that Boyd's gridiron career began to flourish. Of course, Boyd acknowledges that he didn't just leave his mark during the game.

"I played for one of the gang teams for a couple of years, and it was so tough and rough that we drank wine at the half," Boyd said. "All the games wound up in free-for-all fights. By the time I got to Crozier Tech High School, I was already tough, and I thought I could whip anybody."

Aside from his father, he pretty much could. At 16, the renegade Boyd attempted to fight his father, Sam, in the family's kitchen. But Sam Boyd instantly leveled his son, pinned him to the ground and began pounding him like a meat tenderizer.

"I thought I wanted to fight my dad, but I wound up on the floor real quickly," Boyd said. "He pinned me with his foot, took off his belt and began to beat me with the buckle. I was bleeding, the belt was covered in blood and my mother came running. She said, 'Sam, you're going to kill him, you're going to kill him.' He said, 'I'm trying to, but he won't die.' I was mean and no good for nothing. Thank God I had my life turned around."

Boyd's fortunes first began taking a turn for the better when he finally found a home at Texas A&M. With his reputation coming out of high school, Boyd didn't initially have many collegiate suitors. He contacted Baylor, but the Bears had little to no interest. Several other schools gave him a similar response. After a brief stint at Paris Junior College, Boyd contacted Texas A&M, where head coach Homer Norton was willing to give him a shot. But his stay in College Station was conditional.

"I tried A&M, and they said they would take me," Boyd said. "They also said that if I made the ballclub, I could stay. But they said that if I didn't make the ballclub, I would have to leave."

Boyd obviously did much more than make the team. Playing strong-side tackle, Boyd was a three-time All-Southwest Conference performer and was later named to *Sports Illustrated*'s 25-year All-America team. And in leading the Aggies to a perfect 11-0 record and the 1939 national championship, Boyd was selected to six All-America teams. He also earned the praises of perhaps the most famous sportswriter of all time, Grantland Rice, as the '39 Aggies recorded six shutouts and allowed only one opponent—Tulane in the Sugar Bowl—to score more than seven points in a game.

"But even as good as I was on the football field, I was still one ornery, sorry guy off the field," Boyd said. "There wasn't a whole lot to do in College Station back then. But if there was trouble to be found, I was usually in the middle of it. I was a real mess."

Perhaps the toughest man ever to play for the Aggies, Boyd is no longer raising hell. For the last six decades, his singular purpose in life has been leading people to heaven. The Rev. Joe M. Boyd has started numerous churches and a youth camp—Mt. Salem Revival Grounds in West Union—in 1976 that is valued today at roughly $1.5 million; he's preached the gospel around the world; he has authored approximately 15 Christian books; and he has trained hundreds of men in evangelistic, pastoral and missionary work through the years.

"I'm still preaching revivals, and I still preach a full schedule," Boyd said. "I work out of Hyles-Anderson College in the Chicago area, and I have a home in West Virginia, but I miss Texas because Texas is the greatest state in the world. But I've held revivals all over Texas, I have held revivals in Jerusalem, I've been in every state in the union, and I've been in many foreign countries in the name of Jesus Christ. I have been in almost all the Spanish-speaking nations. We preach to so many people in Mexico—5,000, 4,000, 6,500. It's been a real blessing. I have had all kinds of wonderful experiences. I did the revivals in Jerusalem, and they told me I couldn't baptize my converts. I asked them why, and they told me that the Arabs—the Palestinians—would kill them if they were baptized. So I didn't baptize them, but I had a great many people saved. God's been good, and my life's been an adventure. I am living proof that God can save even the sorriest, meanest men if they just ask Him into their heart."

Boyd's heart forever changed after he left Texas A&M in 1940. Even with a cracked neck, Boyd was drafted by the Washington

*Although he was once a self-proclaimed hell raiser, Joe Boyd has spent the last six decades leading people to God. The Rev. Joe M. Boyd has started numerous churches and a youth camp, he's preached the gospel around the world, he has authored approximately 15 Christian books, and he has trained hundreds of men in evangelistic, pastoral and missionary work. (*Photo courtesy of Joe Boyd*)*

Redskins. But after doctors strongly advised him not to continue his playing career, Boyd went to work in the Galveston shipyards.

Boyd wasted little time in rising to the top at Todd Galveston Dry Docks Inc., a company controlled by the Rockefeller family. In a short time, Boyd was placed in charge of all the accounting, payroll, bookkeeping and auditing for the shipyards. But as Boyd rose to the top of the corporate ladder, he became increasingly involved in the numerous temptations Galveston provided in the early 1940s.

"I was bad," he said. "I was drinking, gambling, whatever. The higher I went in sports and business, the more I thought of myself and the less I thought about God or anyone else. I bought into all the good publicity I was getting for boxing, football, wrestling and whatever. I was on the verge of being totally out of control."

Boyd says he first heard God calling him when a hurricane blew through Galveston, tearing the roof off Todd Galveston Dry Docks Inc. while he was inside the building. He heard an even louder voice following a car wreck in the early 1940s.

"My mother had been constantly praying for me," said Boyd, who has two children, four grandchildren and four great grandchildren. "After years of straying, I finally got a Presbyterian preacher to come to my house, and I asked him, 'Does God have anything for me?' He quoted Isaiah 1:18—the exact same verse my mother had told to me time and time again. I fell on my knees and began to cry for mercy. God gave me mercy. My wife had never seen me as defeated. She had always seen me as the champion, the one in control. She came and knelt beside me and she got saved and I got right with God. I have been going in his name ever since. That was 1943."

By 1947, Boyd had earned a masters in theological seminary from Southwestern Baptist Theological Seminary in Fort Worth, and he received a doctorate of divinity from Hyles-Anderson College in '76. Boyd, who is now a widower, is still as driven and determined today as he was when he started his ministry more than six decades ago. And he is probably just as tough as when he led the Aggies to the national championship with a broken neck.

"If I get to where I can't preach standing up, then I will preach sitting down," he said. "And if I can't preach sitting down I will preach from the bed. God called me to preach, and I intend to end my life on this Earth preaching."

There's little doubt that Joe Boyd will do just that. If a cracked neck couldn't keep him off the football field, no ailment is likely to keep him from his passion at the pulpit.

JESSE "RED" BURDITT

Moments earlier, Jesse N. Burditt had removed his fedora, revealing his receding, grayish-white hair. But Burditt still seemed at least surprised when asked: How did you earn the nickname, "Red?"

"I came by that one naturally," Burditt said with a chuckle. "Believe it or not, there used to be a full head of red hair on top. Now it's either gone or gray."

Even without the carrot top, the 78-year-old Burditt is still colorful enough to live up to the "Red" moniker. The gregarious Burditt has more stories than some libraries and is as friendly as a Labrador pup. He possesses a passion for people, a knack for names and a gift for gab. Perhaps the only thing that Burditt doesn't thoroughly enjoy elaborating on is his own accomplishments. Mention his 2003 induction into the Texas A&M Athletic Hall of Fame, and Burditt instinctively begins poking fun at himself.

"To be able to go into the Hall of Fame is very touching," Burditt said. "By the same token, I am aware that there are two plateaus of the Hall of Fame, and I am certainly on the second one. Right before the induction ceremony, my oldest boy, Jess, told me, 'Daddy, just think— in a couple of weeks you will have your picture up there next to some real football players.'"

Photo courtesy of Jesse N. Burditt

JESSE "RED" BURDITT
A&M Letterman: 1943, 1946-47

Position: Split End, Defensive Back
One of only nine three-sport lettermen in A&M history
Held single-game receiving record (125 yards) for 22 years
Still shares school's bowl receiving records with six catches in 1944
Orange Bowl

But don't be misled by Burditt's self-deprecating jokes. Whether he acknowledges it or not, he was one heckuva football player and an even better all-around athlete. As far back as the official A&M athletic records go, Burditt is one of only nine Aggies to letter in three sports, picking up varsity honors in football, basketball and baseball.

And in December 1943, Burditt and his A&M teammates boarded a train to Miami to cap one of the most surprising and inspiring seasons in A&M football history in the Orange Bowl. In that game against LSU, Burditt set an A&M bowl game record by catching six passes against the Tigers. The record has since been matched by three other A&M players, but it has never been surpassed.

Burditt still vividly recalls the six receptions he made that day. For that matter, there is very little about the entire 1943 season that Burditt doesn't remember in great detail. He's replayed the moments and the magic of that season perhaps a million times in his mind.

Burditt can talk to anyone about virtually anything. But his conversational juices really begin to flow when the 1943 A&M team is the subject. Lead him down that path, and Burditt's eyes twinkle like a strand of Christmas lights.

"Outside of my wife, family and my coaching career, playing on the 'Kiddie Korps' team was probably the greatest thing to ever happen to me," Burditt said. "We waited 50 years and then had a reunion in '93. We had our 60th reunion [during the 2003 season]. We had a squad of 72 that year and had 27 here for the reunion, and I keep in touch with 39 of them. The rest of them, we either can't find them or they are dead. But it was certainly a very special team. What most people find hard to believe is that we weren't surprised that we were that successful. No matter the circumstances, it never entered our minds that we weren't going to be good."

It entered the minds of virtually everyone else, though. Most sportswriters believed the '43 Aggies were destined for a devastating season, labeling the Aggies in the preseason as "the beardless boys of Aggieland" and a "glorified high school team." One writer even asked A&M head coach Homer Norton if the Aggies might be better off by following the lead of Baylor and sitting out the '43 season altogether. "Definitely not," Norton said at the time. "If I can find 11 boys on this campus who will suit up, we will have a football team."

The Aggies had established themselves as one of the nation's elite programs by winning the national title in 1939, claiming a SWC co-championship in '40 and winning another outright conference title in '41. But that began to change on December 7, 1941, when the attack on

Pearl Harbor brought the United States into World War II. For the all-male military school in College Station, war would bring about many changes.

Among them was A&M's status as a football powerhouse. Through the Army's A-12 program and the Navy's V-12 program, thousands of A&M upperclassmen were drafted into officer training schools. By the spring of 1943, the A&M football roster was decimated by the draft. In fact, only one varsity player from the Aggies' 1942 roster returned for the '43 season.

"I came here in '43, and that was the year they cleaned out all of the upperclassmen because of the war," Burditt said. "But here's the thing that is really interesting. If you were an upperclassman and a football player, you weren't going overseas directly. They sent you to college for a couple of semesters first.

"So, all of these other schools—Rice, Texas and so forth—that had A-12 and V-12 programs would recruit the best players. We didn't have those programs at A&M. And ol' [Earl] Red Blaik really cleaned up at Army, picking up guys like Doc Blanchard, Glenn Davis and Aggies like Marion Flanagan, Bill Yoeman, Hank Foldberg and Goble Bryant. Military bases also picked guys up, and they played against college teams, too. Randolph Field in San Antonio had 16 All-Americans on its team. And when we played Rice in 1943, there were seven guys on that team that had been playing at A&M in 1942. Practically all of our upperclassmen were gone."

But in the true spirit of the 12th Man, Norton solicited what remained of the Corps of Cadets for football tryouts. When practices began in late July of 1943, 130 youngsters showed up. The average age of the 1943 Aggies was only 17.5 years old. But even as the sportswriters snickered, Norton's Aggies began pulling off upsets. By the time A&M pulled off back-to-back road upsets at LSU and TCU, the Aggies were 4-0 and developing some legitimate star power.

"We just believed we were supposed to be good because we were Texas Aggies," Burditt recalled. "And for me personally it was a dream come true to be playing for the Aggies. My father was class of '21. From the day I can remember the only thing I ever wanted to do was go to Texas A&M and play football. But coming out of Abilene High School [where he graduated at midterm], I arrived at A&M in the spring of '43 thinking I had no chance to play. I didn't even come to spring practice because I weighed only 158 pounds. But that summer [Norton] put an article in the paper saying that he needed football players. I was pretty cocky and said, 'Hey, give me a uniform and I think I can make your

Jesse "Red" Burditt and his wife, Elinor, have remained extremely active in the Bryan-College Station community through the years, and Burditt, who turned 78 in 2004, still goes to the office every day in his role as a financial planner and independent insurance agent. (Photo courtesy of Jesse N. Burditt)

football team.' I wasn't very big, but I had run a 9.7 in the 100-yard dash in high school. And I had a burning desire to prove I could play."

Burditt and the rest of his teammates did just that, and heading into the regular-season finale against Texas, the Aggies were 7-0-1. With the SWC title on the line against Texas, Burditt amassed a school-record 125 receiving yards against the Longhorns. Texas ultimately prevailed, 27-13, but the second-place Aggies, who had become known as the "Kiddie Korps," were still extremely attractive to the bowl representatives. The Aggies accepted a bid to the Orange Bowl for a rematch with LSU, where Steve Van Buren proved to be too much for A&M to handle. Van Buren rushed for two touchdowns and passed for another as LSU beat A&M, 19-14.

By 1944, many of the key contributors of the Kiddie Korps had been "drafted" into other lend-lease programs. After also playing basketball and baseball during his freshman year, Burditt wound up playing football for North Texas Agriculture College in 1944 and then was shipped to Pearl Harbor in 1945. After serving his country as a radio man in Hawaii, Burditt returned to College Station to finish his degree in physical education and marry his high school sweetheart, Elinor. He lettered again for the Aggie football team in 1947 and '48 and also earned a varsity letter on the baseball team in 1948.

He then coached high school football for 12 seasons, compiling a 75-42 record and three district championships while at Hamlin (just outside Abilene), Lockhart and Bryan High. He says that if he had not been so competitive, he might have spent his entire professional career in coaching.

"I loved high school football, and I still love it," said Burditt, who has two grown boys, Jesse III and Charles, and four grandchildren, two of whom graduated from Texas A&M. "But I quit in 1960 because I had asthma so bad in the fall from stress. I was my worst enemy. I just couldn't stand to lose. I got asthma attacks in September, and it wouldn't be until Christmas that I got over them."

When he hung up his coaching whistle for the last time, Burditt joined the Jefferson Pilot Life Insurance Company as an agent and financial planner. He unofficially retired in 1991, but Burditt still goes to the office every day, serving his clients as an independent insurance agent and financial advisor.

"The main point for me now is to work with people and to keep on the run," Burditt said. "I'd go crazy and probably drive my wife crazy if I was just sitting around the house."

There's no chance of that. Even without his daily work, Burditt stays busy with his activities. In addition to being a member of various A&M clubs and organizations, Burditt led the charge in 1997 in raising $35,000 from his teammates for a 12th Man Foundation endowed scholarship. The 1943 team is the only A&M squad that has given such an endowment as a team. In fact, Burditt says he is probably in the A&M Athletic Hall of Fame as much for his organization skills as his athletic talents.

"I'm convinced that the '43 team is the one who did this for me," Burditt said of his induction. "My roommate was Bill Geer. About the second year we started having these reunions, Bill said, 'Red, you really ought to be in the Hall of Fame because you lettered in three sports.' I said, 'Yeah, Bill, and I ought to marry Olivia Newton-John, too.' Induction seemed far-fetched. But Bill started nominating me every year and then he got the team to start doing it, too. I think they loved me so much because of all the reunions we had that that is the way they wanted to honor me. But I'll accept it for whatever reason. A&M means everything to me, and that '43 team was something special."

Despite what Burditt may lead you to believe, so is he. He's one in a million, just as the 1943 Aggies were one of a kind.

BOB
SMITH

Texas A&M's lone recipient of the most prestigious honor in college football, 1957 Heisman Trophy winner John David Crow, was raised in Louisiana with little knowledge of Aggie history. So when Crow first arrived in College Station, he didn't have an A&M role model and couldn't dream of filling the shoes of the legendary (fill in the blank).

But that changed as soon as Crow began watching film of Bob Smith knifing through tacklers and plowing over defenders en route to record-setting numbers.

"When I saw film of Smith, I was really impressed," Crow said. "I never got to watch [1939-40 All-American] John Kimbrough play, but I heard enough about him and saw enough film of Smith for them to be the standard of excellence by which I measured myself. Those were two pretty good guys to idolize for a young running back at A&M. I figured if I could ever be as good as Bob Smith, I would really be something special."

Rest assured, Smith was something special, and he is still the standard of excellence for all A&M running backs in at least one category. Smith left A&M in 1951 as the all-time leading rusher in school history with 2,415 yards. Half a century later, 10 players have surpassed Smith's career yardage totals. But to this day, no A&M player has ever surpassed

Photo courtesy of Texas A&M Athletic Media Relations

BOB SMITH
A&M Letterman: 1949-51

Position: Running Back
First-team All-America running back in 1950
Holds school's single-game rushing record with 297 yards against SMU
Set then-SWC record with 1,302 rushing yards in 1950
Fourth-round draft pick of Cleveland Browns in 1952

Smith's remarkable one-game performance on an unforgettable autumn afternoon in 1950.

In leading the Aggies to a 25-20 victory at SMU, Smith dismantled the Mustangs and amassed 297 rushing yards. During regular-season games, no Aggie has ever come within 60 yards of matching that monumental mark. At the time, the Cotton Bowl in Dallas was well known as the "House that Doak Walker Built." But for one day, Smith made it his personal stomping grounds.

Ironically, Smith didn't know at the time that his performance had been so spectacular. All he really cared about at the time was that he had led the Aggies to a victory and he had made a lasting impression on one SMU coed in the crowd. The summer before the 1950 season, while Smith was taking summer school classes at the University of Houston, he met a pretty, outgoing girl named Betty Lu, who was a full-time student at SMU. The two began dating in the summer, and by the fall they were an item.

Prior to the opening kickoff against SMU, Smith was shagging punts during warmups when a ball bounced toward the stands and landed—as fate would have it—close to where Betty Lu and her friends were sitting. When Smith went to retrieve the ball, he caught a glimpse of Betty Lu. They didn't say anything to each other, but she smiled at him, providing all the motivation Smith needed.

"It was the first time we'd seen each other right before a game," Smith said from his home in Dallas. "She was sitting with all her friends from SMU, and I just went out there and did my best to show off for her. But I honestly had no idea I rushed for 297 yards. In those days, statistics weren't as readily available and there wasn't a lot of information in the Bryan-College Station newspaper. It wasn't until a week after the game that I found out I had set some kind of record. It's pretty amazing, especially with all the great running backs Texas A&M has had, that the record still stands. Heck, I didn't know I had done anything special. I had two or three runs of 60 yards or so, but most of my carries seemed like they were for two or three yards. During the game, it didn't seem so impressive."

But Betty Lu was certainly impressed. A year later, she married Smith during his senior year at A&M, and the couple celebrated their 52nd wedding anniversary in 2003. To this day, she is quick to boast about her boyfriend's sensational performance against her alma mater.

"It was so exciting that I could hardly stand it," Betty Lu said. "I, of course, was rooting for the Aggies because of Bob. But even my friends from SMU began rooting for Bob as the game progressed. He still says he was just trying to show off for me, and it worked."

It worked wonders for the 1950 Aggies, as well. The win over the Kyle Rote-led Mustangs enabled the Aggies, who were just 1-8-1 in 1949, to secure their first bowl berth since the 1943 season in the Presidential Cup in Washington D.C. The SMU game also helped Smith become the first A&M All-America running back since Kimbrough in 1939-40. For the season, Smith rushed for 1,302 yards, establishing a then-Southwest Conference record. And as impressive as he was during the 1950 regular season, Smith may have been even better in the Aggies' 40-20 victory over Georgia in the Presidential Cup.

He set the tone for that game by returning the opening kickoff 100 yards for a touchdown and added an 81-yard scoring run as the Aggies jumped to a 33-0 halftime lead against the nation's No. 1 defense. Overall, Smith accounted for 303 all-purpose yards, which still ranks as the top performance in A&M bowl history.

"That game was a lot of fun, and we just got hot," Smith said. "We sure didn't expect to get up on them 40-0 [early in the third quarter], especially since they were so good defensively. But coming into that game, I don't think Georgia players and coaches thought much about little ol' Texas A&M. They probably didn't pay us much respect. But as the final score indicated, we had a pretty good football team."

The following year was not as glorious for the Aggies or Smith. Harry Stiteler was replaced as head coach by Ray George prior to the start of the '51 season, and the Aggies dropped from 7-4 in 1950 to 5-3-2. Despite a season-ending win over Texas, A&M was left out of the bowl picture.

"I really enjoyed my time under Coach Stiteler, and I thought he was a very good football coach," said Smith, whose rushing totals dropped to 419 yards in 1951. "But honestly, I can't really say the same thing for Ray George. I'm not really sure he knew what he was doing."

Even though his numbers dropped dramatically as a senior, Smith was drafted in the fourth round by the Cleveland Browns. But instead of heading to Cleveland, Smith went to Korea to fulfill his required military duties. After serving two years in the Korean War, Smith returned home to learn that his NFL draft rights had been purchased by the Detroit Lions. Smith then joined Doak Walker and former A&M teammate Yale Lary in Detroit, helping the Lions to the 1953 NFL title.

But after just two seasons in the Motor City, Smith made a decision to leave the game for financial reasons. He had a good job in the off season with an oil field company in Houston, and the Lions were paying

Bob Smith and his wife, Betty Lu, enjoy another moment in the spotlight in this photo from November 3, 2002 at Detroit's Ford Field. Smith, shown here in his old Lions No. 36 jersey, was on hand as Detroit honored the members of the Lions' world championship teams of 1952 and '53. (The couple now resides in Dallas. Photo courtesy of Bob Smith)

him only about $10,000 per year. So Smith gave the team an ultimatum: Pay him more or say goodbye.

"They weren't willing to pay more, so I left," Smith said. "It's kind of ironic when you see what today's players are making that I had to leave the NFL because I couldn't support my family. But I had a wife and two little boys I had to support. I loved playing football, but my first priority was my family."

After leaving football, Smith and a friend opened up a small lumber company in Houston. He then went to work for Millwhite Mud Company, serving as an engineer on inland barges and oil rigs in the Gulf of Mexico. He later moved into sales and joined distinguished Texas A&M alumnus Clayton Williams at Maverick Mud, another service business for oil companies. Then in 1980, Smith decided he had worked for others long enough. He found a print shop in Dallas, and although he had no previous experience in the industry, he decided to go into business for himself.

He bought the Kwik Kopy Shop, changed the name to Downtown Printing and Copy Center, and has been running the business ever since. In 2003, he sold the company, but for the immediate future, the 74-year-old Smith will continue to serve as an active partner in the print shop. "I've enjoyed this line of work and have enjoyed working for myself," Smith said. "And I think we do excellent work."

That's about as close to "bragging" as you will ever hear from the unassuming Smith, who is as down to earth as an oak tree's roots and as accommodating as a bed and breakfast. He has never felt comfortable talking about his own accomplishments. In fact, Smith was so modest about his athletic achievements that even his sons, Barton and Ricky, knew very little about their father's record-setting days at A&M or his career with the Lions. When Barton first began playing organized football, he told his coach that he wanted to play in the "background" like his father.

"I never wanted them to feel like they were pressured to follow in my footsteps," Smith said of his children, who are now in their early 50s. "If they wanted to talk about it, I would let them bring it up. But I didn't want to coach them or push them into anything that they didn't want to do."

Barton, Smith's oldest son, would eventually play football at SMU. Although Smith never pushed the game on his sons, there were many times when he did his best to help his boys—at their request—succeed on the field. He would show them different techniques and even once requested film from Texas A&M.

"Bob is so modest that he didn't talk to the boys about what he had done, but once he was trying to stress the importance of being a great blocker," Betty Lu Smith recalled. "Bob said, 'It doesn't matter how good you are as a runner; you have to learn how to block.' He wanted to show Bart how to do it and asked A&M to send him some films of him playing. Well, they sent him film from the Texas Tech game, which happened to be the one game where he did all the wrong things. Bob said, 'That's what I get for trying to relive the glory days.'"

In spite of his modesty, Smith admits he does take pride in the fact that several of his A&M records are still in place. Most of all, though, Smith says he's proud to be an Aggie.

"I still get chills when I hear the 'War Hymn' and see the Corps marching," said Smith, who once served on A&M's athletic board of directors. "The university and community have gone through some incredible changes since I was going to school. But what impressed me most about Texas A&M way back then still impresses me today. I liked the people an awful lot, and I still do. I'm proud of what the school stands for, and I was proud to have been a part of that football team. I can thank Texas A&M for a lot of good memories."

Likewise, Texas A&M can thank Bob Smith for perhaps the greatest single-game memory in Aggie football history. And as the lone Heisman Trophy winner in A&M history can attest, Smith's legacy impacted the program long after his playing days concluded.

JACK
LITTLE

Back in the late 1940s and early '50s, when websites were the home of arachnids and big brother was actually a sibling, the NCAA watchdog was more of a poodle than a pit bull. And, believe it or not, it was not uncommon for institutions of higher learning to provide student-athletes with—how should we phrase this?—preferential classroom assistance.

The "assistance" often tended to be much more than academic advising. If an athlete could pass or make 'em miss on the field, he was sometimes allowed to miss classes and still receive passing grades. At least during times of high stress. Like, for example, September through May. But most schools absolutely, positively drew the line at giving out passing grades to student-athletes who didn't even play at that particular institution. Most schools. But apparently not all.

Take the case of Jack Little. In 1952, Little became the second lineman in Texas A&M history to be selected to two All-America teams. By that time, the University of Houston had finally figured out that Jack Little was no longer playing football for the Cougars or enrolled in school.

In fairness to UH, Little did enroll as a freshman at Houston. But he never played a down and never attended a single class. After he and

Photo courtesy of Jack Little

JACK LITTLE
A&M Letterman: 1950-52

Position: Offensive Lineman
First-team All-America lineman: 1951 and '52
All-Southwest Conference lineman: 1951 and '52
Fifth-round draft pick of the Baltimore Colts in 1953

his two high school buddies from Corpus Christi discovered that Houston was going through three-a-day practices, they immediately caught a bus to College Station.

"We had visited TCU, and then we enrolled at Houston," said Little, an All-America lineman for the Aggies in '51 and '52. "We were talking to some of the guys in the dorm and one of the fellas was commenting on how hot it was out there and that they were working out in the morning, in the afternoon and at night. One of my high school buddies said, 'Let's get out of here and go to Texas A&M.' I said, 'Where's that?' But we got there and got a tryout for the football team, and I started going to school. You have to understand that times were different back then, and not every school was above board. But when the first grades came out, my mother got reports from both A&M and the University of Houston. She was totally confused as to where I was. I was really working hard at A&M on my school work, but the funny thing is that as I got to figuring out the grades, I was doing better at the University of Houston than I was at A&M."

Perhaps that was the literal definition of "two schools of thought." But by 1950, most everyone who followed college football in the Lone Star State knew where Little was attending school. A&M's opponents certainly did. He was one of the lead blockers for Bob Smith in 1950, when the Aggies led the Southwest Conference in total offense and whipped Georgia, 40-20, in the Presidential Cup. After Smith graduated, Little may have been the most recognizable player on the A&M roster. Not only was he an All-American, but he became the one person who never left the field.

"I remember one year when they started doing the substitutions with the offensive team and defensive team," said Little, who now lives in the Waco area. "I vividly recall we played one year there in Arkansas and fortunately the weather was cool, because I stayed on the field the whole time. All the others would run off. The offensive team would come out and I'd play offense. Then they'd run off, and I'd play defense. I stayed out on the field by myself when they were changing. I guess I should have been honored, but I was really just tired. Of course, I didn't know any better."

Little also didn't know anything about Texas A&M when he first arrived in College Station. All he knew was that football was his chance to make a better life for himself. His father had died when Little was 12, and his mother moved to Washington D.C. some time later, leaving Little and his older brother on their own in Corpus Christi. The two brothers laid carpet for an income until Little's brother received a scholarship offer to play football at Rice. To a young Jack Little, that seemed like the ticket to a better lifestyle. The problem for Little, however, was that he was only a second-team All-District player in high school.

Nevertheless, he was offered a tryout at A&M by head coach Harry Stiteler, who was immediately impressed by Little's toughness, determination and intelligence. Not just on the football field, either. By the time he was a senior at A&M, Little was not only a two-time All-American on the field; he was also on the list of distinguished students. And yes, he did go to classes at A&M and earned every one of his grades.

"Because of my family situation, I felt like my back was against the wall," Little said. "This was my chance to do something. I probably had the ability to do something in high school, but I wasn't using it in high school. I was interested in fishing and running around and just having fun on the coast. It became more important to me when I had my back to the wall, when I had to make a decision on where I wanted to go and what I wanted to do with my life. Truthfully, I didn't even know about education. I knew about school, but I'd never been counseled. I remember that first year at A&M, the coaches were saying, 'All you boys who know what you want to study, get in the different lines. If you don't know what you want to study, come with me.' That was the physical education line, so that's where I went. It was just interesting enough to where I became pretty interested."

Little had other interests at A&M, as well. He married his high school sweetheart, Nancy, at the end of his freshman year, and by the time he left A&M, he and Nancy had the first of their two daughters. The Little family then moved to Baltimore, where Jack had been selected by the Colts in the fifth round of the 1953 draft. He played two seasons in Baltimore before a serious back injury ended his promising career.

"Growing up, I didn't even know there was such a thing as pro football, so it wasn't like I was counting on it or anything like that," Little said. "But once I ruptured a disk in my back and couldn't play any more, I felt like I had my back against the wall again. Football was all I knew."

Fortunately, Little also knew some people in football. After he left the Colts, he was offered a job as an assistant at Texas A&I (now Texas A&M-Kingsville). Soon after, he was offered an assistant's job at Baylor by John Bridgers, who had been an assistant at Baltimore. Little joined Bridgers's staff in 1963, and he immediately helped the '63 Bears to a top 20 finish. Little stayed on Bridgers's staff until 1968, and after Bridgers

Jack Little and his wife, Nancy, celebrate her retirement from the Texas Education Agency in this photo. After he left the Baltimore Colts, Little served as an assistant coach at Texas A&I, Baylor and Sam Houston State before going to work in the state parole system. (Photo courtesy of Jack Little)

was fired, Little stayed at Baylor in the school's outdoor education program.

It was at that time that Little began competing in marathons to quench his competitive thirst. But football would once again call, and Little answered. He returned to the coaching profession at Sam Houston State, where he was working until another back injury convinced him to leave the profession. He then went to work in the state parole system, where he stayed for 17 years until he retired in 1996.

Little, who was inducted into the Texas A&M Athletic Hall of Fame in 1982, now spends his time playing tennis and devoting as much quality time as possible to his family, which includes two daughters (his oldest received her doctorate degree from Texas A&M), a granddaughter and a two great-grandsons. And he and Nancy celebrated their 54th wedding anniversary in August 2004.

"I've been very fortunate, and I have had a lot of blessings," Little said. "Looking back, I really enjoyed my time at Texas A&M, and it helped to shape my life for the better. Football was something in my life, but it was not everything. I just used it to help me get ahead. I'll always be grateful to A&M for giving me that chance, and I still love that school. As I get older, being part of the A&M Hall of Fame means more and more to me. I didn't know anything about A&M when I came to school there, but I'm certainly glad that my buddies talked me into leaving Houston and giving A&M a try. I know A&M was great for me, and hopefully, I gave a little something back."

Little did much more than that. By the time his collegiate career ended in 1952, Little easily fit the description as the Aggies' "big man on campus."

BILL SCHROEDER

Even some five decades later, you're expecting to hear some serious dirt about the legend. You figure that once you bring up Bear Bryant's name, you'll detect the outrage in his voice—or at least sense the lingering resentment. You're prepared for all the juicy details of the heart-felt hatred.

Then the interview begins. It's quickly evident that you're wrong,and Bill Schroeder is as forgiving as Billy Graham. The successful lawyer and former Texas A&M lineman still recalls the afternoon of September 6, 1954, but there are no grudges. And he certainly harbors no ill will toward the man responsible for his near-death experience on the parched practice field in Junction.

"I can truthfully and honestly say I never hated him," Schroeder said from his law office in Lockhart. "Not then, not now. Life is too short for that. But I will say I was greatly disappointed at what I was told happened when I went down."

The truth of the matter is that Schroeder doesn't even remember how it all unfolded. Not the worst part, anyway. But just hearing about it is enough to make the blood of most men boil in fury.

Six days into Bryant's infamous and hellacious survival camp in Junction, Schroeder was 15 pounds lighter than when he had first

Photo courtesy of Cushing Memorial Library

BILL SCHROEDER
A&M Letterman: 1953-54

Position: Offensive Lineman
Member of the famed "Junction Boys"

arrived. He was weak, dehydrated and past the point of exhaustion toward the end of that afternoon's practice.

But Schroeder's uncle had played for the legendary Homer Norton at A&M in the late 1930s, and Bill had dreamt of playing for the Aggies his entire life. No amount of heat, whether produced by the scorching sun or the volatile Bryant, would cause him to quit. So Schroeder pushed forward as the conditioning phase of practice began. Time after time, Schroeder and his teammates ran down the field to cover punts, then ran back to where they started, huddled up and did it again. No breeze, no water, no mercy.

"I was exhausted, but we had not completed that drill, so you continue to work as hard as you possibly can and devote as much effort as you possibly can to that particular drill," Schroeder recalled. "That's what I was doing. Apparently, I went down the field to cover the punt, and, at that end of the field, I basically collapsed. I went to the ground. That's as much as I remember."

Schroeder's internal auto pilot took over, as he pulled himself off the ground and made it back to the huddle. Unconsciously, he broke the huddle and began heading toward the line of scrimmage once again when he tripped and toppled into the drought-ravaged dirt. Schroeder's face began turning shades of purple and gray. His heart raced, producing somewhere between 250 and 300 beats per minute. Schroeder endured a severe heatstroke, and it was time for somebody to do something to prevent him from dying.

At that moment, Bear Bryant did something—something appalling. Bryant kicked Schroeder hard enough that the thud could be heard from 50 yards away. Then Bryant instructed A&M trainers to "Get this [expletive] big ox off the field and out of my sight."

That's exactly what Billy Pickard did. Pickard, now the senior associate athletic director for facilities at A&M, raced Schroeder to a clinic in town, where a Junction physician, John "Doc" Wiedeman, packed Schroeder in ice. Schroeder doesn't remember the kick, the frantic ride to the clinic or the initial moments of having his body packed with ice like a side of beef. In fact, he didn't even initially realize the serious nature of his condition.

"I was coming in and out of consciousness, and I kept wondering why there were soaking wet sheets around me," Schroeder said. "But as I look back, I am so thankful to Doc Wiedeman and his nurses. If you do not reduce the temperature quickly enough, then you're going to have severe, permanent damage to your body and your brain. It could also result in death. I was very fortunate he was able to get my temperature down and under some control within a short period of time so that I did not suffer brain damage, although at times I think my wife probably claims I have some."

Schroeder has no problems joking about the incident today. But his parents were certainly in no laughing mood when they heard about the entire episode. At Bryant's insistence and against Wiedeman's advice, Schroeder was taken back later that same day to the Quonset huts that served as the team's headquarters. Meanwhile, his parents were on their way from Lockhart to bring their boy home. But Schroeder was a warrior. And even after being told what had happened, he wasn't about to quit.

"[My parents] got to Junction, and they were primarily interested in my well-being," Schroeder recalled. "I was told that Coach Bryant did not meet with them, and that was probably for the best. But I was bound and determined that I was not going to leave that team. I'd made up my mind that I was going to hang in there. After they brought me back out to the camp, I was not able to participate in any of the drills. I was in one of those bunk beds, and they would bring me liquids and things like that. I was really weak, but I wasn't going to quit."

Amazingly, Schroeder came back to College Station with his teammates—one of only 35 survivors from the original 115 who had begun the camp. Even more amazingly, Schroeder missed just one game that season—the 1954 opener against Texas Tech.

But what Schroeder soon learned was that enduring a heatstroke of that nature made him much more susceptible to the heat. So Schroeder was often packed in ice on the sidelines of practices and games. Enduring the dismal 1-9 season of 1954 was grueling enough for everyone, but Schroeder's condition made it particularly tough for him.

He needed an extended break to recuperate, so he asked Bryant to be excused from spring practices that preceded his senior season in 1955. Bryant's answer hurt him much more than the kick the head coach had delivered.

"I pleaded with Coach Bryant to allow me to lay out the spring," Schroeder said. "I was completely exhausted mentally and physically. My mother was also having a difficult time because our family doctor in Lockhart said I shouldn't be playing. Coach Bryant said he would not allow me to sit out and come back in the fall because if he treated me like this, he'd have to treat everybody else that way. It was very disappointing, because I wanted so badly to play my senior year. But I knew what I had to do for my health. I couldn't risk my life like that so soon. I real-

Bill Schroeder, shown here with his wife Kay, daughter Mari-Margaret and son Trey, still struggles with heat-related issues, but has long since forgiven Bryant for his actions on that day. (Photo courtesy of Bill Schroeder)

ized it simply wasn't meant for me to play that year. It wasn't going to happen and I accepted it."

Schroeder left the team and never was able to enjoy the thrill of turning the program around. The Aggies went 7-2-1 in 1955 and 9-0-1 in '56, with Junction survivors playing key roles in leading A&M back to respectability.

Meanwhile, Schroeder struggled for many years simply to play a full round of golf because of the heat-related problems. But he certainly didn't spend time sulking. Schroeder moved forward, receiving his law degree from Texas in 1963 and going to work for Congressman Jake Pickle later that year. Schroeder served as a legislative assistant and met his wife, Kay, during Pickle's first campaign for Congress. By 1965, Schroeder was married and practicing law in Lockhart.

Today, Schroeder and his wife have two grown children, Mari-Margaret and Trey (class of '95), and they own a title company in Lockhart. His professional career has been an outstanding success, and in some ways, Schroeder says he can attribute some of that success to the tenacity he displayed in Junction.

"I learned some things about myself out there, and I proved to myself then that even under the toughest circumstances, I could stick to the cause," Schroeder said. "Mainly, though, when I look back I am just thankful. I was blessed to survive. The Lord was there with me. I have thanked God many times. I believe God has given me the opportunity to do some things, even though they may not all be grand and glorious, but He has given me the opportunity to play some part in the well-being of my family, my friends and community, especially my church. I think I've been a more caring person because of that realization."

When the time came, Schroeder even displayed that caring nature toward Bryant. On May 18, 1979, during a 25-year anniversary of the Junction trip, Schroeder zeroed in on Bryant and did what he had been waiting for years to do. Without saying a word, Schroeder found Bryant and wrapped his arms around the legendary head coach, giving him a Bear hug, so to speak.

"He told me, 'Billy, I wasn't sure if you were going to hit me or hug me,'" Schroeder said of Bryant. "I'm really glad that occurred, and I think he felt the same way. And when he died, I didn't have to wish I had let him know how I felt. I never held a grudge."

By the end of the interview, you expect Schroeder to say something like that. He wasn't a big-time star for the Aggies, but he is obviously a bigger man than most of us could aspire to be.

TOMMY MAXWELL

Tommy Maxwell's forearms dot with goosebumps as he recalls Texas A&M's incredible 1967 season. A safety and receiver, Maxwell played a critical role in the Aggies' miraculous turnaround that season, as A&M rebounded from an 0-4 start to win the SWC title and upset Alabama in the Cotton Bowl.

"That season shows you what can happen if you work through tough times," said Maxwell, who still beams with pride at the mere mention of 1967. "The whole key was we never lost faith."

That's also been the whole key to Maxwell's life. Keeping the faith is much more than a season's motto to Maxwell; it's served as his lifelong mission statement. And the reason for the wave of goosebumps on Maxwell's outer layer and the rush of adrenaline swimming through his veins has more to do with what Maxwell now realizes than what he experienced in 1967. Looking back on that year, along with many other events in the more than three decades that have transpired since then, Maxwell clearly sees how it was all part of a master plan.

"I can see how God has used every experience in my past, including all that took place in my life in 1967, to get me ready for what I am doing today," said Maxwell, the founder and executive director of Dallas-based Coaches Outreach, a non-profit Christian organization dedicated

Photo courtesy of Tommy Maxwell

TOMMY MAXWELL
Texas A&M Letterman: 1966-68

Position: Wide Receiver, Defensive Back
First-team All-SWC wide receiver: 1967
First-team All-America defensive back: 1968
Second-round draft pick of the Baltimore Colts in 1969

to the spiritual development of high school coaches and their spouses. "When you see God's hand in everything, it sends chills down your spine. I have a file in my office filled with letters from coaches saying how our marriage retreats saved their marriages. I have countless stories of how our Bible studies have completely overhauled the lives of the coaches we work with. The average coach who coaches 25 years in Texas will coach and teach 22,000 students. No one even comes close to a coach in terms of influencing kids. We're making a difference. And again, I just can't tell you how moving it is to me to look back on my life and see how God has positioned me every step of the way, beginning with my days at Texas A&M."

Maxwell arrived at A&M in the mid-1960s, joining a program that had compiled a measly 11-34-5 record from 1960-64. But by the time he had completed his collegiate eligibility, the Aggies had capped a remarkable championship season and Maxwell had become a two-way star. He earned first-team All-SWC honors as a receiver in '67 and was recognized as a first-team All-American as a senior safety in 1968. He then became Baltimore's second-round draft pick in 1969 and was part of the Colts' Super Bowl V championship team in 1970. Maxwell also spent three seasons with the Oakland Raiders and finished his NFL career in 1974 with the Houston Oilers, when a neck injury forced him to retire.

But for all the glorious moments he experienced in football, Maxwell says the most memorable, life-altering moments that took place in his life during that time happened away from the field.

"I accepted Christ my junior year at A&M," Maxwell said. "Growing up, I went to church probably twice a year, so I knew about Jesus and said the Lord's Prayer every night, but then I would go out and live like I wanted to. But at A&M, there was a man named Prof Smith who taught me the Bible and led me to Christ. And then after I was done playing at A&M, I was really disappointed that the Dallas Cowboys didn't draft me in the first round. But that also turned out to be a blessing because the Colts drafted me. Bob Vogel, a Pro Bowl player and a leader on the team, immediately asked me if I would like to go to the Bible study on Friday night. Friday night is the party night for most pro players. But there were six or seven guys on that team, including Bill Curry, Bob Vogel, John Williams and Jerry Logan, who were in that Bible study group. Those guys really helped to shape me and strengthen my faith."

When his football career ended, Maxwell returned to College Station and worked for the Texas A&M Development Foundation, where Maxwell says he developed a thirst to learn more about the Bible.

During his time at the A&M Foundation (1974-78), Maxwell began teaching Bible studies for students and athletes in dorm rooms, and he started an adult chapter of the Fellowship of Christian Athletes in College Station. His passion for sharing God's word led him to Dallas Theological Seminary and then on to a church in Georgetown, where Maxwell served as a pastor for three years.

Philosophical differences with several powerful members of the church eventually led Maxwell out of the ministry and into the insurance industry. It also left him wondering if he had made a mistake in comprehending God's message for his life.

"When I left the church I was a worn-down pup," Maxwell said. "I guess you could say I was fired, and I was asking God why I was in the insurance business. Looking back, now I can tell you exactly why, because it really helped bring some discipline in my life and gave me an understanding of how to run Coaches Outreach. It also helped me in my business skills and communication skills, teaching me to talk to business leaders and promote our benefits, which is one of the things I do today with Coaches Outreach. But it was while I was selling insurance that a high school coach called me up and asked me if I would come and teach a Bible study he was getting going. We met at the Texas High School Coaches Association Building in Austin every Thursday morning. That was in January of 1987, and that's probably where you could say that Coaches Outreach unofficially began."

By 1990, that Bible study had attracted numerous coaches in the Austin area and had become so beneficial to the participants that Maxwell decided to introduce a weekend marriage retreat into the curriculum. Maxwell's first marriage retreat attracted 18 coaches and their spouses. The retreat, which encouraged coaches to form their own Bible studies and stressed the importance of the coaching profession, was a major success. Word of its impact quickly spread across the state. The second retreat in 1991 attracted 40 couples—the maximum capacity at the time—and a waiting list began for the next one. And with each passing year, the numbers have continued to grow. In the summer of 2004, for example, the Coaches Outreach retreat attracted 315 couples.

Those increasing numbers are a confirmation of sorts to Maxwell. In 1993, he left the insurance business and went to work for the Dallas Theological Seminary in its advancement office. While Maxwell continued to organize and oversee the marriage retreats from Dallas, his time became more and more scarce. By 1995, Maxwell had put together an advisory board for the retreats and organized two retreats per year. And in 1996, he hired a secretary to work part-time on organizing the

Tommy Maxwell (far right) opened the doors of Coaches Outreach, a Bible-based ministry designed for coaches and their wives, in 1997. Maxwell's ministry has saved numerous families from divorce. Maxwell's own family includes (from left) wife Janice, daughter Lezley, son-in-law Patrick Nugent, granddaughter Kate and daughter Lauren. (Photo courtesy of Tommy Maxwell)

retreats. But even then, Maxwell believed he was being pulled in too many directions.

"I got busier and busier with my work at the Dallas Seminary, and after the retreat in '96 I told the coaches that this was getting too hard for me," Maxwell said. "They didn't want to hear that and told me that this could be a full-time ministry. We got to talking about the idea of starting Bible studies across the state. But I honestly wasn't sure. I had a good job, and I was 50 years old then. I began talking it over with my wife and praying about it, and when God wants you to do something, you'll do it. After a while, the Lord convinced me of the importance of these coaches, and I thought, 'Let's go for it.' I just told the seminary that this was something that I had to do, and I didn't know how it was all going to work. But those coaches believed in me, and God brought a few people into my life and gave me the sense to realize that He was going to take care of me. It wasn't a lot of money, but it was enough to meet our needs, and He has never forsaken us."

On May 21, 1997, Coaches Outreach opened its doors in Dallas with one full-time employee: Maxwell. Since then, Coaches Outreach has started more than 80 new Bible studies in communities across the Lone Star State. Maxwell is no longer a one-man operation, but he still wears plenty of hats.

Among other duties, Maxwell writes the organization's newsletter, writes the Bible study material, meets with businessmen about possible funding, drives across the state to start Bible studies, plans for retreats and everything else he can manage in a day.

"We write our own material, which is very coach-specific with questions that apply to them," Maxwell said. "It is a verse-by-verse study of the Bible, so the coaches really learn the Bible and see how it applies in context to them. It is more of a study than a devotional. We have been dead serious with our message. We are not here to fool around or play games. We want to help reach coaches and have coaches reach not just kids, but also other coaches. These coaches become accountable to one another through a small group. It is a word-of-mouth ministry, and we are not out there to see how big we can get. It is not easy to start a Bible study. We want to get one going and make sure it stays going, so it is something the coaches can look forward to year after year. We're not going to get rich, but we're certain we are answering a calling. This is all about spreading God's word to coaches, so that they can positively influence kids. If we can help these coaches to be better role models, then we are going to have a positive impact on the kids. Obviously, we feel like it's a very good cause."

Perhaps there is no better cause. And perhaps there is no better man for the cause than Maxwell. His lifelong passions have been faith, family and football, which all fall under his job description.

STEVE O'NEAL

According to the small-town legend, former Texas A&M coach Gene Stallings pulled into a Hearne gas station in 1965 and began discussing Aggie football personnel needs with the service station owner, who was also an avid fan of local high school football. While he was pumping gas and checking under the hood, the owner casually informed Stallings that the best punter in the Lone Star State was already enrolled at A&M.

Noticing that he'd piqued Stallings's interest, the owner explained that he had watched Steve O'Neal, who was then an A&M freshman on a track scholarship, punt when O'Neal played at Hearne High School. Stallings then paid for his petroleum and promised his new pal that he would follow up on his tip.

So, in essence, Stallings pulled in for gas and left with the knowledge of a player who would help fuel A&M's run to the 1967 Southwest Conference title. At least that's how the story goes.

"I'm not so certain that's actually how it happened," said O'Neal, who has served as a dentist in Bryan since 1976. "Coach Stallings did approach me during the second semester of my freshman year and asked me about trying out as a punter. But Ken Batson [O'Neal's high school coach at Hearne] may have just called Coach Stallings and told him

Photo courtesy of Texas A&M Athletic Media Relations

STEVE O'NEAL
A&M Letterman: 1966-68

Position: Punter
First-team All-SWC punter in 1967
First-team All-America and All-SWC punter in 1968
13th-round draft pick of the New York Jets in 1969
Holds record for the longest punt in NFL/AFL history

about me. There are actually several versions of the story, but the gas station version does make for a much better story."

Regardless of which version is correct, O'Neal's career as a punter at Texas A&M and in the pros makes for a fascinating—if unlikely—success story. From virtually out of nowhere, O'Neal emerged as the Aggies' punter in 1966, helped A&M to the '67 title, became an All-American in 1968, was drafted by the Super Bowl champion New York Jets in 1969 and set the all-time record for the longest punt in professional football history later that year.

Not a bad football career for a high hurdler/long jumper who really wasn't even the first-team punter at tiny Hearne High School.

"I played end, defensive back and punted some in high school, but I certainly never envisioned a football career the way it turned out," said O'Neal, who played four professional seasons with the Jets and one year with the New Orleans Saints. "We had several good punters in high school, and one of them happened to be the coach's son. He was also a very good running back, and I didn't really start as a full-time punter until the coach's son got hurt during my senior year. But I had a few good punts when I got my chance."

They were at least memorable enough to leave a lasting impression on the service station owner. And true to his word, Stallings did follow up on the tip. Stallings contacted A&M track coach Charlie Thomas, who informed O'Neal that the Aggies' second-year football coach wanted to speak to him. When O'Neal arrived at Stallings's office, A&M's head coach told assistant coach Elmer Smith to take the kid onto the field for a tryout.

"If he really can punt," Stallings told Smith at the time, "come back and get me."

The rest is rather remarkable history. O'Neal earned a roster spot after his initial tryout and then averaged 42.3 yards per punt during the 1966 season. A year later, the NCAA implemented a new rule that prevented any members of the punting team from releasing downfield until after the ball was kicked. So, working with Smith, O'Neal developed the Rocker Step. As the ball was snapped back to him, O'Neal would rock backward. Then, when he caught the ball, he only needed to take one step before punting. Normally, punters take at least two steps before they kick.

"With the Rocker Step, the ball would usually be gone within about 1.8 to two seconds after it was snapped," O'Neal said. "It was very effective for me, and it really helped out the team as far as getting down on punt coverage. I used it for the rest of my career at A&M and for one or two years in the pros."

O'Neal didn't just use the Rocker Step; he transformed it into an art form. In 1967, he led the Southwest Conference, averaging 42 yards per punt, as the Aggies claimed their first SWC title since 1956 and won their first bowl game since 1950. One year later, O'Neal was selected as a first-team All-American after averaging 40.9 yards per punt. To this day, O'Neal and Shane Lechler are the only A&M punters ever to be selected as a first-team All-Americans.

O'Neal left A&M as the second leading punter in school history based on his career average of 41. 8 yards (he's now tied for fourth on the list). But even as glorious as his unexpected collegiate career had been, the best was still yet to come for O'Neal. He was selected in the 13th round of the draft by the Jets in 1969, and after beating out incumbent punter Curly Johnson in training camp, the former Hearne High back-up was starting for the defending Super Bowl champs.

In the second game of the '69 season, O'Neal and the Jets visited Denver's Mile High Stadium to face the Broncos. In a close game, the Jets started a possession at their own 20, but quarterback Joe Namath was sacked twice during the series, and O'Neal was called upon to punt.

"To be perfectly honest, I thought Joe was sacked in the end zone the second time," O'Neal recalled. "I thought it was a safety and I was going out there to do a free kick. But as I started out there, I noticed the official was marking the ball inside the one-yard-line."

At the time, the goal posts were located near the front of the end zone, adding further intrigue to a tight situation. So O'Neal positioned his feet against the back line of the end zone and slightly to the right of the goal post's nearest upright. He then instructed upback Matt Snell not to back up and told himself, "Just hit it good."

He did much more than that. The ball sailed over the head of Denver's return man, traveling about 75 yards in the air. Then, when it hit at the Broncos' 35, it bounced like a bad check, rolling all the way inside the Broncos' one-yard line. The stunned Broncos return specialist eventually caught up with the ball, but by the time he picked it up, the Jets' coverage team swarmed on top of him at the one-yard line.

Officially, it was listed as a 98-yard punt, the longest ever in the NFL or AFL. Ironically, O'Neal says he has hit the ball better than he did that day. But he's never seen such a perfect roll, taking off at impact with the ground and slowing to a stop just as it approached the opposition's goal line.

After his career in pro football, Steve O'Neal returned to Bryan-College Station in 1976 to open his dental practice. O'Neal, pictured here with his family— (from left) Lindsay, Judy and Lesley—still resides in the community where he first became a star at Kyle Field. (Photo courtesy of Steve O'Neal)

"The most amazing thing to me is that, all these many years later, people still bring it up all the time," said O'Neal, whose wife later had the shoe he wore that day bronzed. "The first question they usually ask me is, 'Was there a blizzard of a wind at your back?' Or, 'Was it because you were in that thin air?' First of all, there was almost no wind. Secondly, the air may have had something to do with it, but I've kicked the ball further than that—in the air—down here in the thick, humid air. I kicked probably 80 yards a couple of times down here in practices. But that particular punt was just one of those unforgettable things where everything worked our right. There's really no explanation for it."

O'Neal's wife, Judy, begs to differ. Judy and Steve grew up near each other and went to Hearne High School together, but they had never been more than friends and had never gone on a date until the week before that Jets-Broncos game. Judy received a job offer in New York at about the same time the Jets drafted O'Neal, and since she didn't know a soul in the Big Apple, she called O'Neal on September 17, 1969—four days before the Jets' game in Denver.

"You could barely even call it a date, because she was just bored and lonely when she gave me a call," O'Neal said. "I was about to walk out the door of my place in Flushing Meadow for the city, so I drove over to her place and took her to Broadway Joe's just so we could talk and catch up on old times. I then took her somewhere else where I introduced her to my roommate and some friends. That was it. But that's where it all started, and we've been together ever since. She, of course, says she was the inspiration for that 98-yard punt. She might be right."

The O'Neals obviously possess the right chemistry, which may have something to do with Steve O'Neal's lifelong fascination with sciences such as chemistry. Even in high school, O'Neal knew he wanted to be involved in science, eventually deciding that he wanted to be a dentist. In fact, O'Neal was already enrolled in the University of Tennessee's dental school when he was drafted by the Jets. And throughout his professional football career in New York and New Orleans, O'Neal continually went back to dental school during each off season.

When push came to shove, O'Neal even chose dentistry over football. After four seasons in New York, O'Neal was traded to the lowly Saints, where he played one year and was twice voted the most valuable player of the week for New Orleans. But in the 1974 preseason, he tore cartilage in his knee and was forced to undergo an operation. By the end of the '74 season, he received another chance to return to the game when the Dallas Cowboys offered him a free agent tryout. But at the time, he was just nine weeks away from completing his dental school work.

"I was never really the same after the injury," he said. "Even when Dallas called, my knee was hurting and my back was hurting. I didn't know if I was in shape to make the team, and since I was so close to graduating from dental school, I decided, with only minimal regret, to say 'no' to the Cowboys. We were ready to move on with our lives."

They were also ready to move back to Central Texas. Steve and Judy O'Neal considered settling down and opening a dental practice in big cities like New York and New Orleans. They considered medium-sized cities across the country, as well. But the Bryan-College Station area felt most like home, and they have been in Aggieland since 1976, raising their two daughters, Lindsay and Lesley, in the shadows of Kyle Field.

Lesley O'Neal, 24, graduated from Texas A&M and is now in Los Angeles pursuing an acting career, while 26-year-old Lindsay was married in May 2004 and is now a nurse in Denver—the same city where her father made the most historic punt in professional football history.

Although he stays busy with his practice, O'Neal says he always finds time to follow the Aggies. And although he is quite humble about his role on the 1967 title team, he's extremely proud to be a part of one of the most memorable years in A&M football history.

"That was a lot of fun, and that was probably the highlight of my collegiate career," he said. "It's something I'll never forget and will always be proud of. It's kind of funny how things worked out. I never expected to be remembered as a football player or even to be a football player. But I'm sure glad it worked out like it did."

It all worked out like it did because Gene Stallings stopped at the right service station when he needed a fill-up. Or so the story goes.

Where Have You Gone?

BUBBA
BEAN

Sitting on the tailgate of a tool-filled, equipment-loaded pickup truck, Bubba Bean takes care of the dust on his hand and the sweat on his forehead with one quick brush of the brow. Aside from the sprinkling of gray in his goatee and the tingling in his surgically repaired knees, Bean still looks and feels much the same as he did when he was terrorizing defensive backs in the Southwest Conference and later in the NFL.

Slender, muscular and as fit as the December day he appeared on the cover of *Sports Illustrated* in 1975, Bean laughs at the suggestion that his exercise routine must be arduous.

"My wife and I occasionally try to walk a little bit," says the soft-spoken but engaging Bean. "But other than that, I have no exercise routine whatsoever. This is what keeps me moving, hopping, sweating and going."

"This" is both his profession and his passion. If you can dream it, explain it or draw it, Bean can probably build it. While some men think in pictures, Bean visualizes in blueprints. Some men dream of supermodels; Bean is consumed by remodels. And his wife, Kathy, who married Bean when he was a freshman at A&M in 1972, is fairly certain her husband's DNA contains at least some traces of sawdust.

Photo courtesy of Texas A&M Athletic Media Relations

BUBBA BEAN
A&M Letterman: 1972-75

Position: Running Back
First-team All-SWC running back in 1974 and '75
Sixth leading rusher in A&M school history (2,846 yards)
First-round draft pick of the Atlanta Falcons in 1976

If there's daylight and a job to do, Bean usually has a hammer in hand or a concrete truck on the way. Bean, who since 1995 has been the owner of Bean Construction, is driven—perhaps even obsessed—by the satisfaction of jobs well done. As his reputation for meticulous, high-quality construction continues to grow throughout Central Texas, Bean has more jobs than ever before in Bryan, College Station and the surrounding areas.

Bean Construction basically started off as a one-man operation. But Bean now oversees several crews and at least 10 employees, including his son, Jarrett, and his son-in-law Robert Cooks, who is married to Bean's daughter, Nicki. Bean still prefers to renovate or remodel residential properties, but he is also willing to tackle commercial endeavors such as the African-American Heritage Museum in downtown Bryan, for which Bean served as the general contractor.

"I specialize in work—any work—and we try not to shy away from anything," Bean said. "We enjoy the physical side of it, and I certainly enjoy being out here working with my hands and building projects that the owner can be proud of and that I can be proud of, as well. I have been doing this for a full-time living since 1995, but I've also been doing stuff in construction since I was about 12—even during off seasons. It's something I enjoy doing, something I find very therapeutic. Then I saw an opportunity to do it full-time and get out of the rat race. I can see a sense of accomplishment every day when I leave a project. I love it. I can't emphasize that enough."

Bean has experienced the sense of construction satisfaction before. He was, after all, instrumental in the reconstruction of Texas A&M football some three decades ago. Bean was part of Emory Bellard's first recruiting class in 1972 and helped the Aggies go from SWC also-rans to national championship contenders during his four seasons. For the most part, the Aggies have been Top 25 mainstays ever since, which is a source of pride to Bean.

"It is meaningful to me because somebody had to make the first move to come to A&M," said Bean, still the sixth leading rusher in A&M history with 2,846 yards. "I came here the same time as Ed Simonini, Garth Ten Naples, Carl Roaches, Richard Osborne, Pat Thomas and that group. What's ironic is that if Colorado had gotten back to my house before A&M, I would have signed with Colorado. But my mom and my dad, who did not want me to go out of state, kind of intervened and called R.C. [Slocum], who was recruiting me at the time. What's also ironic is that I was with R.C. the day he took the A&M assistant job. He was recruiting me for Kansas State at the time, at his brother's house in Orange, Texas. We're sitting out in the yard, and he got a phone call from Emory. He walked in and came back and said, 'Well Bubba, you know all that stuff that I was telling you about K-State? Forget it. Think Texas A&M.' I didn't know what the future would hold, but it turned out to be a really good move for me."

Good for the Aggies, too. In Bean's first two seasons, A&M struggled to records of 3-8 and 5-6. But by the start of 1974, it was apparent that Bean and the rest of Bellard's first recruiting class would form the nucleus of something special. In Bellard's Wishbone offense, Bean led the Aggies with 938 rushing yards in 1974 as A&M posted its first winning season in seven years. Then, in 1975, things truly came together as A&M rolled to a 10-0 start and a No. 2 national ranking with one game left to play.

Following the 1975 win over Texas, Bean appeared on the cover of *Sports Illustrated* under the headlines that read: "A&M stakes its claim. Bubba Bean shreds Texas."

Bean is still the only Aggie ever to be featured on the magazine's cover. On the down side, however, he can also speak with authority on that strange phenomenon known as the "*Sports Illustrated* jinx." Thanks in large part to the nation's stingiest defense and No. 44 on offense, the Aggies looked as if they might have a shot to win it all in '75. But shortly after Bean appeared on the *SI* cover, Arkansas pummeled an emotionally drained A&M squad, 31-6, costing the Aggies a shot at the national title and an outright SWC title.

Bean, who again led the Aggies in 1975 with 944 rushing yards, admits he has replayed that game in his mind. But it no longer causes him the anguish that it once did.

"I learned a long time ago that you can't go back and dwell on things," Bean said. "I don't jump off the deep end simply because I lost a football game, even when it might have meant as much as that Arkansas game. If we had won that game, it might have changed some things for A&M's future. But on the other hand, it's not the cure to cancer that we've all been looking for. I don't lose sleep over it."

Following the disappointing end to 1975, Bean was a first-round draft pick of the lowly Atlanta Falcons. Along with quarterback Steve Bartkowski, also a first-round selection in 1975, Bean helped the Falcons reach the playoffs in 1978 and again in 1980. Both playoff trips, however, were ended by heartbreaking losses to the Dallas Cowboys. In the latter loss, the Cowboys overcame a 24-10 fourth-quarter deficit and won on a dramatic Drew Pearson reception in the corner of the end zone.

Since 1995, Bubba Bean has been the owner of Bean Construction in Bryan-College Station. The ultimate handyman who will tackle virtually any construction project, Bean is shown here on a job site with his son Jarrett Bean (left) and son-in-law Robert Cooks (right). (Photo courtesy of Rusty Burson)

"The second loss [to the Cowboys] pretty much reminded me of Arkansas," Bean said. "Pearson made a catch just like the Arkansas receiver caught that fluke pass over Lester Hayes just before halftime in college. It just kind of fizzled out from there."

Bean played a couple more seasons of pro football and eventually moved back to the Bryan-College Station area in 1986. He began working in the athletic department under Jackie Sherrill and then moved to career planning and placement, where he stayed until 1995.

Bean says he enjoyed working with the university, but he was just not a desk person. Bean had an itch for construction that wasn't being properly scratched by his weekend projects. So he decided to start his own business in 1995, and it has been growing ever since. Interestingly, Bean says his athletic connections did help him in starting his new business.

"When I went back to work for the university, [former athletic director] Wally Groff was the first person I did some construction work for. He asked me what I had been doing since I quit playing football. I told him and he said he had some work at his house. I wound up doing some work for him and then Penny King, his secretary at the time, said she had some work at her house she wanted done. It kind of snowballed from there."

Now, it's practically an avalanche. In fact, Bean is so busy that he can barely keep up. At one time, Bean's payroll included about 15 employees, but he has cut back over time because of too many administrative headaches. The bottom line is that Bean never wants to grow his business so large that he begins taking shortcuts or loses his ability to take part in the actual construction process.

"I never want to get too spread out, because I enjoy the hands-on part too much," he said. "Besides, it's already extremely time-consuming. There is a big misconception that because you have your own business you have a lot of free time. My wife gets on me from time to time because I work too much, but in order for this to be successful you have to put in the time. I said when I got into this that I was willing to do what it took to get it up and running. Hopefully, in another couple years, I will let my son and son-in-law take over the business, and I'll show up at 10:30 and see how it's going. I just turned 50 [in early in 2004], so I'm looking toward a time when I might want to slow it down a little and spend a little more time with my granddaughter, Madison, and on the golf course."

Not too long ago, Bean maintained a 5 handicap on the golf course. But as business has continued to increase, Bean's golf time has continued to decrease. It's a sacrifice Bean says he can live with for the time being.

"It's a good thing I do love construction as much as I do," Bean said. "I'd be awful miserable if I didn't love it, because I'm out here from sun up to sun down on most days. The key for me is that I don't get stressed about my work. On the contrary, I find it very enjoyable. It's not for everybody, but it's great for me."

And obviously great for his physical conditioning. His focus now may be on adding square feet, but Bean still looks as if he could pile up the yards.

Where Have You Gone?

TANK MARSHALL

Coming out of Oak Cliff's Roosevelt High School, Charles "Tank" Marshall once entertained about as many collegiate football options as a Saturday afternoon satellite dish viewer. Marshall could choose from among 60 different scholarship offers, including numerous programs with a winning track record.

Instead, Marshall chose Texas A&M, which in 1973 was coming off a 3-8 season and had not produced a winning record since 1967. Marshall did not have family ties to A&M, and he didn't possess a particularly extensive knowledge of A&M's football potential or history. What weighed most heavily on Marshall's mind when selecting A&M was a childhood vow he made to himself and his family.

While Marshall grew up in the Dallas area, his father's childhood home was Navasota. As a result, the Marshall family was on the road from Oak Cliff to Navasota more times than virtually anyone in the family can possibly recall. It was during those regular trips that Tank Marshall first began envisioning himself at Texas A&M. And it was in the back seat of his parents' car that Marshall first vowed to be an Aggie. His parents didn't give it much credence at the time, but Marshall never forgot.

Photo courtesy of Texas A&M Athletic Media Relations

TANK MARSHALL
A&M Letterman: 1973-76

Position: Defensive End
First-team All-SWC defensive end 1975 and '76
1976 Aggie Heart Award winner
Third-round draft pick of New York Jets in 1977

"The program was not rolling, and let's just say that there wasn't a lot of kissing going on back then," said Marshall, who now resides in Arlington. "But it was a dream come true for me to go to A&M. Before the outer loop of Highway 6 was constructed, you had to come right by campus to get to Navasota. I would look over and see the big campus and the huge administrative building, and as a 10-to 12-year-old, I would always tell my parents, 'I'm going to go there someday.' They just figured I was some babbling youngster who had been in the car too long. But lo and behold, as God and fate would have it, I got the chance to come here. It was really special, because I had always wanted to go to school at A&M."

Marshall, 49, turned out to be an extremely special player at A&M, too. He anchored a remarkable defense that helped the Aggies compile a 28-7 record from 1974-76. An All-Southwest Conference defensive end in 1975 and '76, Marshall was a reckless, havoc-wreaking force up front, playing a major role in the Aggies' finishing the '75 season as the No. 1 defense in the country. Marshall still takes pride in that No. 1 ranking. But it's the "one" that slipped away that still brings a grimace to his face.

The '75 Aggies rolled to a 10-0 start and were ranked No. 2 nationally with one game left to play. The school's first national championship since 1939 seemed to be within the Aggies' grasp. But a made-for-TV decision changed the date of the Arkansas game, moving it from November to the first weekend of December. After the emotional victory over Texas, the Aggies showed up in Little Rock a little flat. They left flattened, as Arkansas rolled to a 31-6 win in what can probably be considered the most disappointing loss for A&M in the last 30 years.

"From a playing standpoint, the 1975 season sticks out most in my mind, but it is both a sweet and a bitter memory," Marshall said. "I have no doubt in my mind that if we would have beaten Arkansas, we would have gone to the Cotton Bowl, beaten Georgia and won the national championship. But as it turned out, we went into Arkansas and didn't get it done. It was an all-or-nothing game, and we pretty much ended up with nothing. That's still disappointing to me."

But in some way, that loss also turned out to be a valuable lesson in life for Marshall. Although he didn't realize it at the time, he would be forced to bounce back from a series of disappointments in the years to come. Following the 1976 season, Marshall was drafted in the third round by the New York Jets, but a knee injury cut his first shot at the NFL short. He rehabilitated the knee and signed in Canada to play with the Winnipeg Blue Bombers for two seasons before leaving the game.

Marshall was married with a child on the way and the bills mounting, so he returned to Dallas and took a job first at a pipe plant and then in a warehouse. He was making a living, but it was all by the sweat of his brow. One day, in particular, made him reconsider where his life was heading. While working in a furniture warehouse, an 18-wheeler pulled up to the dock at approximately 4:40 on a Friday afternoon. The driver wanted the truck's contents—refrigerator-freezers, couches, monstrous tables, etc.—unloaded immediately. Marshall tried to explain to the driver that the forklift was broken, while his supervisor made a beeline to the loading dock.

"All I had was a two-wheel dolly," Marshall recalled. "The supervisor saw the truck and came down to me, and he put his arm on my shoulder and said, 'We don't need a forklift; we have Charles here, and he will be able to do it.' Well, I had a wife, and I was living with my mother-in-law. I had to do what I had to do, but that really sticks out as a turning point in my life, making me focus on going back to school."

Before he went back to school, though, Marshall gave the NFL one more shot, earning a tryout and then a contract with the Houston Oilers. Marshall was enjoying an extremely impressive training camp and was receiving a number of indications that he would make the team. But once again, a serious knee injury derailed his plans. After another knee surgery, he went back to hard labor on an offshore drilling rig. That's when he finally started listening to the voices from the past.

"I got to the point," Marshall said, "where I was thinking, 'This isn't cutting it.' I started hearing the voices from coaches and teachers I had before saying, 'You have more potential than this. You need to finish school.'"

That's exactly what he did. He set out a plan to replace some of the failing grades on his transcript and then re-enrolled at Texas A&M. While going back to school, Marshall also worked as an academic/athletic advisor during the Jackie Sherrill regime. He earned his degree in 1986 with only one regret.

"Because of my size at that age, I've been known as 'Tank' ever since fifth grade," he said. "It was even 'Tank' on the Aggie Heart Award. I couldn't get it put on my diploma, though. I really tried, but these folks are very serious about what name goes on the diploma. I still use my nickname to this day, especially with Aggies."

Once he graduated from A&M in '86, Marshall left his blue-collar work uniform behind for good. And during the last 18 years, he has made a rapid ascension up the corporate ladder by applying the same energy, intensity and focus to his career that he once displayed on the

Charles "Tank" Marshall married his high school sweetheart, Chandra. The couple's youngest son, Josh, is a promising two-sport star in Arlington. The Marshalls' oldest son, Kevin, is not pictured here. (Photo courtesy of Charles Marshall)

football field. He is now the public water team leader for the Texas Commission on Environmental Quality, covering 19 counties in North Texas. In essence, Marshall is ultimately responsible for the public drinking water in all of those counties.

He is also the proud father of two outstanding athletes, 23-year-old Kevin and 17-year-old Josh. Kevin Marshall, who was drafted by the Texas Rangers in the 20th round coming out of Arlington Martin High School, played junior college baseball, while Josh is a football and baseball standout at Martin. Only a junior, the six-foot-two Josh is already earning the attention of college coaches as a receiver. But he also happens to be an outstanding baseball prospect, as well—due in large part to the countless hours Tank Marshall spent with his two boys on the baseball diamond.

"Watching them grow up, I really made a point to work with the boys and spend time with them," said Marshall, who has been married to his high school sweetheart, Chandra, for 30 years. "Many A&M alumni, like Bob Frymire, Bum Bright and others, told me about how they made their fortunes the hard way. They worked their tails off, but they all said it took them away from their families. So I have always made it a point to work hard, but also to spend quality time working, coaching and just enjoying my boys."

Marshall acknowledges it would be another dream come true if his youngest son proves to be capable of playing at Texas A&M. But regardless of whether that happens or not, there may not be a better ambassador for Texas A&M than Charles "Tank" Marshall. Over the years, he has returned to campus numerous times to speak to the football team—first under R.C. Slocum and most recently at the request of Dennis Franchione—and to provide some sage advice about the benefits of finishing school the first time through.

It's good for the players to hear. But it's also good for Marshall to come back. Just as he felt many years ago while driving past the campus in his parents' car, Marshall has a sixth sense that he is where he belongs when he is back in Aggieland.

"I just get a special sense when I come back here of peace," he said. "I feel at home here. I don't feel rushed. It's just a good, healthy feeling of being at home. No matter your ethnic background, religion or whatever else, when you're here, we're all Aggies. I say that very sincerely. This place has always been special to me, and it always will."

MARK DENNARD

During Mark Dennard's collegiate career at Texas A&M, the Aggies compiled a 36-11 record, attended three bowl games, shared a conference title and developed a reputation as a top 20 mainstay. As a co-captain in 1976 and an All-Southwest Conference center in '77, Dennard was a key ingredient in the Aggies' recipe for success. Of course, Dennard may now be an equally successful crowd pleaser among A&M faithful because of his more literal recipes.

Just ask the thousands of patrons who believe that no weekend visit to Bryan-College Station is complete without stopping at one of Dennard's three Wings 'N' More locations. For many current and former students, the restaurant has become a staple in the local landscape, and it may now rival the Dixie Chicken as a must-experience destination for first-time visitors.

Its atmosphere is authentically College Station and undeniably Texas A&M. Even though Dennard opened his first Wings 'N' More in Houston and first conceived of opening a restaurant that specializes in buffalo wings while living in Miami, his College Station locations could only be more A&M-oriented if Reveille roamed the restaurants and assumed the duties of the tiny towlettes that are now passed out to patrons dripping with wing sauce.

Photo courtesy of Texas A&M Athletic Media Relations

MARK DENNARD
A&M letterman : 1974-77

**Position: Offensive Lineman
First-team All-SWC center: 1977
A&M's first-team All-Decade team of the 1970s
SWC's second team All-Decade team of the 1970s
10th-round draft pick of the Miami Dolphins in 1978**

"When I was in Miami playing for the Dolphins, we had our own little party lot outside the stadium, and after games guys would bring wings out," Dennard said. "We would have a few cold beers and eat those wings. I had never eaten buffalo wings before, but I loved them and asked the guys where these things came from. So, one night they took me to the restaurant in Fort Lauderdale and the place was just packed. I thought that was a pretty good deal. My wife, Donna, didn't like chicken, but I finally convinced her to go with me, and she got hooked just as quickly as I did. Then our kids got hooked. So I asked the owner if they were franchising."

They were, and the rest is culinary history to savor for Bryan-College Station residents and visitors alike. Dennard opened his first Wings 'N' More on Interstate 290 in Houston in 1986 and then opened the first College Station restaurant across from the A&M campus in 1988. In 1994, he opened a second College Station location in Southwood Valley, and in 2003, he opened a massive restaurant on University Avenue that replaced his original College Station location. Business is thriving—especially on football weekends—like never before, as lines often snake out of the waiting area and into the parking lot. Dennard always dreamed big, but the current popularity of his restaurants is even more than he ever envisioned.

"When I opened the first one on 290, from open to close, I was there mopping floors, cooking and doing whatever else needed to be done," said Dennard, who has since sold his original location and one other Houston restaurant to a partner. "I guess I just wasn't smart enough to know what it was supposed to be like and how rough it was in the beginning. But literally, you could have shot a gun off in there and not hit anybody during lunch hour. But I just kept the doors open and kept plugging along. I guess I've seen about a 1,000 percent increase in business from that day to now. We do more business in one day now than we did in the first month that I opened that first one."

Aside from the outstanding taste of the wings, the atmosphere of Wings 'N' More is appealing to all sports fans and caters to Aggies. Televisions are constantly tuned to games, A&M athletes and coaches frequently stop by, and the walls are covered with an impressive collection of sports photos and memorabilia. Many of the photos document Dennard's career and feature signed prints of friends he met during an impressive nine-year NFL career that included a trip to Super Bowl XVII.

Like his restaurants, Dennard was always a local favorite during his NFL career. After leaving A&M, Dennard played seven seasons with the

Miami Dolphins and two with the Philadelphia Eagles and ended his career with the Cleveland Browns. There were memorable moments throughout his pro tenure, Dennard says, but the two that loom largest in his mind came from his first start and his last game.

"My first start came in my second year in the league, and we were playing the Oilers on *Monday Night Football*," said Dennard, a 10th-round draft pick of the Dolphins in 1978. "I was lined up against Curly Culp, and on about the third play of the game he stuck his thumb in my facemask and jabbed me in the eye. It cut my eye, which was about three-quarters shut for the rest of the game. Then, with about four minutes to go in the fourth quarter, he got me in the other eye, and I thought I had a detached retina. I had triple vision in that eye. That was my welcome to the NFL."

His farewell to football was equally painful from an emotional standpoint. After starting for the Eagles in 1984 and '85, Dennard was released by Philadelphia's new head coach, Buddy Ryan. So he wound up back in Miami, but a preseason ankle injury and an attempt to come back too soon earned Dennard a call to Don Shula's office.

"I tried to play without any ligaments in my ankle," Dennard said. "But with about three games to go in the season, Shula called me into the office and said, 'I think you've lost a step.' I said, 'No kidding.' I was going to retire after that year anyway, but I just wish Shula would have let me retire as a Dolphin. But they let me go, and the Browns signed me because Mike Baab, out of the University of Texas, was hurt. They offered me full benefits for the playoffs, and I really liked [former Browns coach] Marty Schottenheimer."

That move almost earned Dennard a second Super Bowl ring. Only one of the most famous drives in NFL history prevented Dennard from at least getting a shot to play on the NFL's biggest stage.

"I was in Cleveland," Dennard said, "when [Denver's] John Elway directed 'The Drive.' Cody Risien, who was a teammate of mine here at A&M, was playing with the Browns, and with about four minutes left in the game, the Broncos had 98 yards to go just to tie the game. Cody was sitting there saying, 'We're going to the Super Bowl.' I told him to hold on, because the fat lady had not sung yet. Sure enough, Elway worked his magic and that was a real disappointment for us. But even looking at it from the other sideline, that was a pretty impressive drive. Unfortunately, that was my last football game. Schottenheimer invited me back to camp the next year, but I just thanked him for the call and decided to retire. My kids were getting older, and I was ready to be back in Bryan-College Station on a full-time basis."

Mark Dennard opened his first Wings 'N' More restaurant in Houston in 1986 and in College Station in 1988. From left, Donna, Mark, Christine and Wes Dennard may be the "first family" of food in Bryan-College Station thanks to the popularity of the restaurant. (**Photo courtesy of Mark Dennard**)

When Dennard first arrived in College Station as a talented prospect from Bay City, he had no family ties to Texas A&M. But after his experiences as a student-athlete in the mid-1970s, he wanted to make sure his own children received the opportunity to become part of the Aggie family. His 24-year-old daughter, Christine, is a 2001 A&M graduate and his 23-year-old son, Wes, who spent a couple years as a walk-on deep snapper, is a 2004 Aggie grad.

"I met my wife when I was at A&M, played on some great teams at A&M and have so many special memories of this place that it was really a great feeling to see my kids go to school here and appreciate A&M for all the school is," Dennard said. "And, of course, I love the fact that some people consider a trip to Wings 'N' More as part of the complete football weekend visit for A&M games. Plus, this is a great community to live in, and the people here have obviously been very good to us."

Likewise, Mark Dennard has also been great for A&M and the Bryan-College Station area. When it comes to local flavor, Dennard obviously has spiced things up.

PHIL
BENNETT

Hours earlier, Phil Bennett watched in anguish and grief as his once-vibrant wife, Nancy, was buried in her hometown of Alvarado. It obviously wasn't supposed to end this way.

The Bennetts were going to grow old together, watch their children grow together, baby-sit grandchildren together. He was the Kansas State defensive coordinator on the rise; she was the inspiration of all his dreams. He was the hard-charging leader of the family; she was the warm-hearted woman who made their house a home.

The coaching profession had taken the Bennetts plenty of places. And there wasn't much doubt that they were going to bigger places together. As long as Nancy was by his side, Phil Bennett figured he could handle anything and possibly conquer any obstacle that stood in his path. She was his everything.

Now, she was gone. A lightning bolt struck Nancy in the summer of 1999, and 14 days later, Phil made the agonizing decision to take her off life support. She died shortly thereafter.

There was no time for preparation, no plans for a different life, no gradual acceptance and no logical explanations. Nancy, 41, went out for a morning jog on the first day of the rest of her life; she never came back.

Photo courtesy of Texas A&M Athletic Media Relations

PHIL BENNETT
A&M Letterman: 1976-77

Position: Defensive End
Second-team All-SWC defensive end in 1977
1995 Division I-A Defensive Coordinator of the Year
(*American Football Quarterly*)
Became SMU head coach in 2002

Now, as Phil and his two children left the funeral and flew back to their home in Manhattan, Kansas, he wondered how he would possibly make it without Nancy. So many questions raced through his mind. How would his kids handle it all? How could he be both a mother and father to them? Could he stay in this time-demanding, stress-inducing profession? Why, Lord, did this happen? Why?

Ever since the lightning bolt jolted his life, Bennett had spent much of his time looking toward the heavens as he asked those questions. But as he was mulling them over again in his mind on the flight back to Kansas, Bennett received what he perceived as a sign from above as he was gazing toward the ground below.

"One of my most vivid memories of the day we buried Nancy in Alvarado is the children and I flying back on a private jet and flying over this stadium in Dallas," Bennett recalled. "It was Ford Stadium, and I'm just looking down—the kids are asleep—and I'm thinking. 'How in the world am I going to do this, how am I going to coach?' Seeing Ford Stadium got me thinking. The job at SMU is one that I always thought could be a really good job. I just looked at it as we flew over and it was almost like he tipped his wing. I had always tried to prepare myself to be a head coach, but I just didn't know if it would ever happen. But I do know it has been a blessing that God's will has led us back here around Nancy's parents and brothers and sisters, and my brothers and sisters. Having Dat [Nguyen] here and so many other people around here to give us support has been a huge blessing."

Bennett became SMU's 15th head coach in 2002, and while everything hasn't gone his way on the field—the Mustangs went 3-9 in Bennett's first year and 0-11 in 2003—the former A&M standout believes he is exactly where he needs to be. In 2003, Bennett signed the school's best recruiting class since the mid-1980s, and he followed that up with another strong class in '04. He also happens to be the head coach of one of the youngest teams in the nation. In 2003, for example, 41 of Bennett's 79 scholarship players were either true freshmen or red-shirt freshmen.

So, despite the disappointing win-loss record, Bennett appears to have the long-suffering SMU program headed in the right direction. Bennett, who earned second-team All-Southwest Conference honors for the Aggies as a defensive end in 1977, acknowledges that turning the Ponies around is not an overnight process. But after what he has been through in his personal life in recent years, he doesn't even bat an eye at difficult jobs.

Bennett knows the definition of difficult. He could write a book on the subject. This, after all, is the man who was forced to tell his kids that their mother was gone forever. That experience gives anything related to football an entirely new perspective.

"There was probably a time in my life when an 0-11 record may have seemed like the end of the world to me," Bennett said. "But the hardest thing I ever had to do was to wake Sam and Maddie up and tell them that their mother had been struck by lightening and it didn't look good. And then the hardest thing was the day I had to tell them their mother had died. It gives you a perspective on life and how short and fragile it is. I still remember it so vividly. She had gotten up that morning, and she was telling me about a conversation she had the night before with Dat. They had talked for a long time, and she said she had better go for a run. A little later that morning, I saw it was raining, and I pulled up to a policeman who didn't have his lights on. I got out and said 'Have you seen a good-looking blonde jogging?' He looked at me and he recognized me and he said, 'Coach, did you know that lady?' It was one of those things where you knew at that point your life would never be the same."

It probably will never be the same. But Bennett has managed to move forward. He's done it for his kids, 16-year-old Sam and 13-year-old Maddie; he's done it in honor of Nancy's memory; and he's realized that he must move forward for himself.

Of course, he is quick to acknowledge that he hasn't done it alone. Bennett says he has received support from numerous sources, including the Aggie family. Both Phil and Nancy graduated from Texas A&M, and both knew Aggies were a special group. But Bennett says his admiration and appreciation for Aggieland continued to rise following his wife's death.

"During that tough time for me the support I received from people going back to when I played at A&M was unbelievable," said Bennett, a native of Marshall. "That support is what gets you through it. So many Aggies, along with the people at K-State, were unbelievable. It's been challenging, but it's also been gratifying watching your kids grow and learn from this. I've learned a lot about myself. I've learned I can do a lot more things than I thought I could. I think I've learned to appreciate people helping me more. I've always known I've been blessed by having good friends, but I just never realized how many people are out there. If you read the paper, you would never think there were any good people left. I'm living proof that people have helped Maddie, Sam and I get through this. As I tell people, we are doing relatively well—not dysfunc-

Since the tragic death of Nancy Bennett in the summer of 1999, the Bennetts—(from left) Sam, Maddie and Phil—have drawn closer to each other and have relied on the support of Phil's extended football family ties. (Photo courtesy of Phil Bennett)

tional—and a lot of things are happening. I'm engaged to a wonderful lady in College Station, Julie White, and there are a lot of things happening that are positive right now."

One of the most positive relationships for Bennett and his kids has been the growing bond the family has nurtured with Dat and Becky Nguyen. As the defensive coordinator for the Aggies in 1995-96, Bennett developed a special relationship with Nguyen. In fact, the leading tackler in the history of Texas A&M football credits Bennett for giving him a chance and teaching him how to play the game at a higher level. Nguyen also credits Nancy Bennett for much of his collegiate development off the field.

"She was like a second mother to me," Nguyen said. "And he was the guy who gave me a chance. If it wasn't for them, I don't know where I would be today. But I am so glad to be here in the same city with them again. Maddie and Sam mean so much to Becky, me and our daughter. We love those kids and love spending time with them. Considering all they have gone through, they are doing great. And I know, beyond any doubt, that Coach Bennett will get the job done at SMU. He knows a thing or two about handling adversity and tackling challenges."

Indeed, he does. Bennett, who has served as an assistant at A&M, TCU, Iowa State, Purdue, LSU, Oklahoma and Kansas State, believes he may be closer to turning things around at SMU than many people think. He has a plan in place, and he says his players have bought into his model for success.

"There are probably still some lingering effects [from the 1987 death penalty], but only if we let them be," Bennett said. "SMU has unlimited potential. It's a challenging job, but we can get this done. I believe we're getting it done. We're in a state that has the best high school coaches and football players in America, and we're focused on recruiting this state. With our new facilities, if we can get them on campus, we have a great opportunity of getting them. I know it's going to take time. None of us are as patient as we need to be. But there will be a day when I believe we can be a top 25 program again."

Until then, Bennett welcomes support from anyone and everyone. He doesn't even mind playing second fiddle.

"I've spoken to A&M clubs, Texas clubs, and I have told them I don't mind being your second team. Dallas is full of people who are from all parts of the country, and if they can't make it back to their own school, we can be their adopted school. I do get a sense that a lot of Aggies are pulling for us to get it turned around. Going through the situation with Nancy and her being an A&M graduate, their affection for me and my family has been unbelievable. I'm so proud of my kids, and I'm so proud to be associated with a place like Texas A&M. My fiancée lives down there, I'm down there quite a bit, and I'm still an Aggie fan. Everything that I could do to help them I would do, and I would like to think they would like to see us succeed. I tell people that A&M is a place that helped me grow up. I am basically watching two teams these days. I watch us and I am pulling for the Aggies."

Undoubtedly, the majority of Aggie fans are also pulling for Bennett. They've seen him endure the worst of times off the field, and they'd love nothing more than to see him experience the best of times on the gridiron.

THOMAS
SANDERS

A t the conclusion on the 1984 football season, Thomas Sanders was presented the prestigious Aggie Heart Award, an annual honor that is voted on by teammates and awarded to a Texas A&M senior who exhibits extraordinary resolve in intangible qualities such as effort, competitiveness, desire, leadership, determination and courage.

Sanders says he was honored that his teammates thought so much of him at the time. But with the benefit of two decades of hindsight, Sanders now believes he probably didn't truly learn about those intangibles until a year after he left Texas A&M and joined the Chicago Bears.

Sanders wound up in the Windy City as a ninth-round draft pick of Chicago, serving as a special teams standout on one of the most special teams in NFL history—the 1985 Super Bowl champion Bears. But perhaps the most personally meaningful role he played on that team was as the backup tailback to one of the greatest running backs in the history of pro football.

Playing behind Walter Payton didn't offer Sanders much playing time, but watching the legend closely did provide a lifetime's worth of lessons about the game of football and the game of life.

"I learned quite a bit from Sweetness," Sanders said from his home in the Chicago area. "And most of what I learned from him came with-

Photo courtesy of Texas A&M Athletic Media Relations

THOMAS SANDERS
A&M Letterman: 1980-84

Position: Running Back
Texas A&M's leading rusher in 1984
Among the top 25 career rushers in school history
1984 Aggie Heart Award winner
Ninth-round draft pick of the Chicago Bears in 1985

out him saying a word. As far as I am concerned, he was the greatest running back to ever play the game. He was an incredible athlete, and he
worked incredibly hard. And what most people really didn't know about
him was how banged up he was all the time. There were many times
when he was too banged up to even practice. His ankles would be
swollen, and he might have fluid on his knees. He could barely walk, but
come Sunday, it was like there was nothing wrong with him. He was an
amazingly tough man on the field, and he displayed that warrior's men-
tality until the day he died."

Payton died on November 1, 1999, after succumbing to bile duct
cancer. Shortly before his death, Sanders visited his friend and former
mentor, receiving the opportunity to say goodbye. Even with Payton's
health failing and his body deteriorating, Sanders says he remained the
picture of class and character.

"He had such an incredible passion for life and for people,"
Sanders said. "He was a notorious prankster, and he was always playing
jokes and pranks in the locker room. He was just so full of life, and he
wanted everyone around him to have as much fun as he was having. I
know this sounds trite and overused, but he was every bit as extraordinary off the field as he was on the field. He was a great family man, a
great man and a great role model who touched so many lives. I will
always be grateful for the time I spent with him."

Payton and the other cast of zany characters on the Bears' 1985
roster treated Sanders to the time of his life as a rookie. The head-bang-
ing, trash-talking, fun-loving Bears ignited a frenzy in Chicago and captivated much of the country as they dominated the NFL and stormed to
a 46-10 win over the Patriots in Super Bowl XX.

Sanders had never played on a playoff team in high school and had
been a part of just one bowl game—the 1981 Independence Bowl—
while at A&M. So winning it all with the Bears as a rookie was as stunning as it was exhilarating.

"Honestly, the other rookies and I were in a daze for most of the
'85 season," Sanders recalled. "But it was definitely something great to
be a part of. When we came back here from New Orleans, I was just
speechless because of the things I saw. When we were coming back from
the airport on the bus to go downtown for the big parade, we were basically the only vehicle moving on the expressway. People got out of their
cars and were cheering us on from the overpass and the side of the road.
You would have thought we had just conquered the world. I was on top
of the bus when we got downtown, and I could see people as far as the

eye could see. Chicago is such a great sports city, and the entire city was nuts about us.

"In fact, the '85 Bears team is still brought up a lot. I think probably the biggest reason for that is that the Bears haven't had many good teams since then. My only regret is that we didn't do more than we did. I would have never imagined that with the players and the nucleus we had on that team that we wouldn't have gone back to the Super Bowl. But it was a lot tougher because everyone was gunning for us, and some of the guys got caught up in their celebrity status. We were on top of the world for one season, but we had the talent to do it for much longer."

Sanders played five seasons with the Bears and two more with the Philadelphia Eagles before leaving the game for good. He considered moving his family back to Texas, but eventually decided to stay in Chicago, where he and his wife, Novaita, are raising their three children—Tiffany, 19, Ashley, 14, and Derrick, 8. Sanders has also been part of several successful business ventures in the Windy City. He was formerly the co-owner of an advertising and promotions company and is now a lease-finance broker for a company that leases items such as construction equipment and computers.

Sanders has lived in Chicago long enough that he considers it home. But he hasn't completely ruled out the possibility of one day returning to the Lone Star State, where he first hit the big-time at small-town Giddings High School. Sanders earned Class 3A All-State honors as a senior and was one of the state's prized recruits as a senior. And 24 hours prior to national letter of intent day in 1980, Sanders recalls that he was 99.9 percent sure he would sign the next day with the University of Texas.

So what happened in a day's time that helped to deliver the future Aggie Heart Award winner to College Station? Sanders now calls it a fortunate twist of fate. Texas simply didn't want to wait a few weeks on Sanders. That turned out to be a decision the Longhorns would pay for in years to come.

"When I first visited Texas, they really put a high-pressure sales pitch on me and wanted me to sign right then. I told them I wanted to wait a little while and make a decision after thinking about it and talking it over. But they never called me back. Some time went by, and my high school coach finally called Texas on the day before I was planning to sign with them to see what the situation was. Texas said they had already signed all the running backs they needed that year. So I was just basically out of luck."

Thomas Sanders and his wife, Novaita, met at Texas A&M and reside in the Chicago area with their three children (from left) Ashley, Derrick and Tiffany. (Photo courtesy of Thomas Sanders)

But not completely out of options. Sanders had visited A&M and enjoyed his trip to College Station. But when the A&M coaches called on him, Sanders indicated strongly that he was leaning toward Texas. Just hours before signing day, however, the roles were reversed. Sanders was calling A&M, hoping and praying the Aggies still had a scholarship to give and an interest in giving it to him.

"I was very, very nervous when I called [assistant coach] Jess Stiles and said I would like to come to A&M," Sanders said. "Fortunately, they had a spot available for me. It's pretty amazing how things worked out for the best from that point forward."

Sanders immediately went from being spurned by Texas to being a thorn in the Horns' side. He scored a touchdown against the Longhorns as a freshman in 1980, helping the Aggies to 24-14 victory in Austin.

And Sanders concluded his collegiate career in '84 with an excellent performance in A&M's 37-12 win over Texas in Austin. That win, combined with the upset victory over nationally ranked TCU in the previous game, helped kick-start A&M's dominant role through the remaining years of the Southwest Conference. The Aggies won the next three league titles and won six of the next nine SWC championships.

"I think we planted a seed by the way we finished up 1984," said Sanders, who led the Aggies with 738 rushing yards as a senior. "To see what A&M did immediately after that made me feel like I was a part of the team that helped turn things around. And it was especially gratifying to beat Texas twice. I got over the fact that they had kind of turned their back on me right away. But I can't deny there was a special satisfaction there in beating them. Looking back at it now, it was a blessing how things all worked out. In hindsight, I wouldn't have wanted to be anywhere but A&M. I met my wife at A&M, and it helped to shape my future in many ways. Despite several frustrating injuries throughout my collegiate career, I was really fortunate with how things worked out. I have so many good memories, and I met some great friends and developed some great relationships throughout my football career."

Indeed, from meeting his sweetheart at A&M to meeting Sweetness in Chicago, and from winning the Aggie Heart Award to earning a Super Bowl ring, Sanders has consistently proven to be a winner in the game of football and the game of life.

SCOTT POLK

A year earlier, Texas A&M had taken a 13-0 lead over Texas as Kyle Field rocked and swayed like rarely before. Could this be the year, Aggie fans thought, that the tide finally turned in A&M's favor?

The answer was a definitive "no." The Longhorns stormed back from the early deficit in 1983 to score 45 unanswered points against the outmanned Aggies en route to a convincing 45-13 win. It was the 12th Texas victory in the last 16 meetings against the Aggies and yet another painful reminder to A&M fans of the Horns' supremacy in the series.

So the following year when the Aggies sprinted to a 20-0 halftime lead over the Longhorns in Austin, few A&M fans were breathing easily. And when Texas marched impressively down field early in the third quarter, there was a fear among many Aggies that "here we go again."

"I'm sure folks in the stands felt that way," said Scott Polk, a senior linebacker in 1984. "Our luck against Texas hadn't been real good. Sometimes the ball bounces your way; sometimes it doesn't. Against Texas, it hadn't usually bounced our way."

This time, however, it did. With the Longhorns at the A&M 10, Texas kicker Jeff Ward lined up for a 27-yard field goal attempt that would have cut into the A&M lead and given the Longhorns a big momentum boost. Instead, A&M's Domingo Bryant swooped in from

Photo courtesy of Texas A&M Athletic Media Relations

SCOTT POLK
A&M Letterman: 1980-84

Position: Defensive End
Hero of the 1984 win over Texas
Signed free agent contract with the Kansas City Chiefs in 1985

the right side to block the kick. Polk, on the left side, picked up the loose ball and lumbered 76 yards to the Texas 7. The Aggies converted the block into an 18-yard Eric Franklin field goal and a 23-0 lead.

The fat lady began singing, while Texas fans began exiting. Texas A&M went on to a 37-12 win, and Polk instantly became a folk hero. It was the type of play that had broken the Aggies' hearts so many times in the past. And it is the play many Aggies still refer to when discussing turning points in the Texas series.

Beginning with the '84 game, A&M rolled off six straight wins over Texas and won 10 of the next 11 against the Horns. Even today, when Polk meets fellow Aggies, the first topic of conversation is usually about the play. Ironically, Polk says, many Aggies now remember it for being even bigger and better than it actually was.

"Never in a million years would I have thought people would still be talking about that play," said Polk, who now lives in Dallas. "One of the funny things is that I see a lot of old Ags that will recall the particular play as a touchdown. They'll say, 'I remember the game in Austin on Thanksgiving, it was on ESPN, where you caught that block, or the fumble, or the interception and ran it back for a touchdown.' Over half the guys that bring it up remember it as a touchdown. I never really bother to correct them."

Polk jokes that it probably should have been a touchdown, but that he was actually just trying to run out the clock.

"I can honestly say I recall some thoughts of what was in my head, the first of which was, 'What's taking everybody so long to catch up to me?' I remember the term 'lumbering' was used to describe it," Polk said. "I don't blame them. I don't think I had run that far since two-a-days. Defensive guys don't run 80 yards for sprints; we run about 40. I was good for the first 40 yards, but after that, I started to lose ground."

Polk will probably forever be remembered by many Aggies for that one play, but he also had an extremely productive career at A&M otherwise. Polk's father, John, graduated from A&M in 1957, so Scott grew up with one primary vision in mind: Playing football at Texas A&M. As a senior at Dallas W.T. White High School, Polk took some other recruiting trips, but he always knew where he would eventually sign.

"I did what a lot of high school guys do, taking their little recruiting trips to see what's out there and to have some fun, but there was never a doubt where I was going," said Polk, who played both defensive end and outside linebacker during his collegiate career. "I remember taking a recruiting trip out to Texas Tech, and they showed us some statue of a guy on a horse and they said his rear was pointed toward College

Station. That actually made me kind of mad. They knew I wasn't headed to Lubbock."

Polk followed his heart and signed with Tom Wilson's Aggies in 1980. He played as a true freshman and even started a few games during the '80 season. He endured a knee injury that spring and was still not 100 percent the following fall. But he played enough as a sophomore to earn a letter before a severe hamstring tear ended his season prematurely. Polk was awarded a medical redshirt for the '81 season, and after playing the next three years, he became one of only a few five-year lettermen in A&M history.

Following his final season at A&M, Polk signed a free agent contract with the Kansas City Chiefs. Polk jokes that if he had only had a little more size and a lot more speed he would have been a perfect fit in the NFL. Instead, he was with the Chiefs for only a couple of months before coming back to Dallas to become involved in the family business.

His grandfather started in the diamond business in the late 1940s, and today, Polk runs the wholesale diamond distributorship from the World Trade Center in Dallas. As president, he oversees the operation and works with various retail stores to place the fine jewelry his business manufactures.

"It has been a rewarding career," Polk said. "It is enjoyable to work with something that is generally going to represent a good time in people's lives. Jewelry is usually a symbol of someone's love for another person, and it's nice to think that what we are producing could become an heirloom and something that they are excited to receive. It beats selling caskets."

Polk is usually quicker with his one-liners than he was with his feet. For instance, he and his wife, Stephanie, celebrated the birth of their third child, John Cody Polk, in 2003. When asked how he decided on the name, Polk said: "I thought long and hard about it, and I figured it would sound good over the public address system in case he ever makes a tackle, a basket or hits a home run. Besides, if you are a spotter in the press box, you would probably be more inclined to give a tackle to a kid named Cody Polk than if we had decided to name him 'Tuiasasopo Polk.' With a name like John Cody Polk, he might wind up with a few more tackles to his credit in the final statistics."

Truthfully, John Cody Polk is named after his grandfather. But the public address angle makes for a good story. Rest assured, his daughters, 12-year-old Shelbi and nine-year-old Becca, have become quite familiar with their father's playful stories. And although Stephanie Polk attended

Scott Polk, who now runs a wholesale diamond distributorship, makes his home in the Dallas area with his family: (from left) Shelbi, Cody, Becca and Stephanie. All the Polks have become well-versed in their father's heroics in the 1984 win over Texas. (Photo courtesy of Scott Polk)

Baylor, she has through the years become quite an authority on the story regarding the play that made her husband famous among Aggie faithful.

"Oh yeah," Polk said. "She's even more amazed than I am that people are still talking about it. I think my oldest daughter has heard about it plenty of times, too. I tell them that they better know all about that one play, because it was probably the only one I made at Texas A&M."

While Polk downplays his impact on the A&M football program, he looks back on his time in College Station with tremendous satisfaction. He was able to fulfill a dream by playing for the Aggies, and he also began some of the most meaningful relationships in his life.

"I feel very blessed to have played college football and to have been at A&M," he said. "I had to have a knee operation, and my wife has asked me, 'Knowing all you know now with your knee, would you do it over again?' I told her I would absolutely do it again. God provided some unbelievable relationships for me and some real growth in my life when I was at A&M. I was blessed to have been involved in a great church down there, Grace Bible Church. The friends that I made and just the experiences I had while I was at A&M have meant so much to my development physically, mentally and spiritually. I wouldn't change a thing if I had it to do all over again."

Neither would many A&M fans, who still vividly recall that warm December night in Austin when Polk helped to finally break the Longhorns' backs.

"Some reporter once wrote that that was the play that changed A&M football," Polk said. "I don't know about that, but it was the start of a lot of years of success against Texas. We went to one bowl in the five years while I was there, and that was the 1981 Independence Bowl. But it did seem like we were building up under Jackie Sherrill. The year after I left, we went to three straight Cotton Bowls. So depending on one's view of life, you could say I was either part of the dead wood or part of building something special. Selfishly, I like to think I was part of the latter."

Objectively, so do thousands of other Aggies who love to recall Polk's rumble as a changing of the pecking order in the A&M-Texas series.

KEN REEVES

Growing up in a tiny East Texas town, Ken Reeves often wondered if the moving truck would eventually arrive in the driveway and deliver the pulpit to his home. With as much preaching as his parents provided, Reeves figured he might come home one day to find the couch had been replaced by pews.

The sermons Reeves continuously heard from his parents had as much to do with higher education as a higher power. Reeves's mother was a teacher for 35 years, and both of his parents were college educated. From the time he can remember, Reeves recalls being educated about the importance of an education on a dizzying basis. Like many adolescents, Reeves welcomed the parental words of wisdom like an acne breakout on prom night. Reeves, after all, was a high school star who had it all figured out. School was simply a means to an end zone. Reeves didn't necessarily believe school wasn't important, but it was a distant fourth to football, basketball and track—the activities he believed would punch his ticket to success.

"My parents preached education with a passion," Reeves said from his office in Houston. "But by the time I was in high school, I believed I was God's gift to football."

Photo courtesy of Texas A&M Athletic Media Relations

KEN REEVES
A&M Letterman: 1981-84

Position: Offensive Lineman
Second-team All-SWC offensive lineman in 1984
Sixth-round draft pick of the Philadelphia Eagles in 1985

He was. At Pittsburg (Texas) High School, Reeves starred in numerous athletic arenas. On fall Friday nights, the entire population of Pittsburg—3,000 strong—would pile into the wooden bleachers to catch a glimpse of Reeves on the rampage. At one point or another in his prep career, Reeves played defensive end, defensive tackle, linebacker, tight end and offensive tackle. He even kicked for a short time. "But I wasn't too good at [kicking]," Reeves recalled.

That's about the only place where he didn't excel. He was rated as one of the top 11 players in the Lone Star State in all classifications as a senior in 1979. USC, Notre Dame, Texas, Arkansas, Oklahoma and practically every other major university in the country drooled over the collegiate potential of Reeves.

When he wasn't thriving on the gridiron, he was starring in other athletic endeavors. Reeves was an All-State basketball player and also pulled off a remarkable feat in track, earning All-State honors in the sprint relay, mile relay, shot put and discus. His athletic prowess made Reeves feel as if he could leap tall buildings in a single bound. It also made it more difficult for Reeves to concentrate on his parents' preaching.

That changed in 1980 when Reeves arrived at Texas A&M to begin what he anticipated as an All-America career. On the first day of his first practice in pads, Reeves's knee ligaments were ripped apart. Suddenly, his parents' sermons came racing back to mind, as Reeves wondered if he would ever play football again.

"It was probably one of the worst things to happen to me, but it was also one of the best because I had to put things into perspective," Reeves said. "I was thinking I was going to walk into A&M, start right away and do this and that. While it's good to have those expectations, you have to be able to keep focus on why you are there. Initially, the scales tipped more toward football than focusing on getting a great education. The injury made me do some soul searching and made me say to myself, 'Hey, you have to buckle down and work like you never have before to even come back from this injury. And you need to realize that your education is the most important thing.' I'm proud I was able to do that."

Reeves now owns two degrees from Texas A&M—an undergraduate and a master's—and is working toward his Ph.D. While he is already preaching the importance of education to his own son, five-year-old Kenneth Wayne Reeves II, he is also intent on becoming a spokesman for African-American athletes at Texas A&M and beyond. His primary incentive in pursuing his Ph.D. is more for motivational purposes than monetary ones. Reeves, an account executive for Countrywide Financial Services in Houston, has enjoyed plenty of personal and financial success. Now, he wants to share his wealth of knowledge.

"It's a shame, especially with African-American athletes, that we are limited to sports heroes," Reeves said. "I want to get the Ph.D. and be able to consider coming back to A&M or going to a different setting to advise or be a role model. With everything you see about athletes getting into trouble, they may need some guidance and may be able to use some direction. The African-American athletes may need someone who looks like them to really receive the message. I've always lived the premise that you need to extract every bit of potential you have within you. I never wanted to settle for being only an athlete. When it's all said and done, I want to look back and say I left no stone unturned. So the Ph.D. is something I want to put in my tool-box to be able to mentor some guys. It will give me a platform where some guys may pay more attention to what I say."

Reeves has plenty of good advice, and the fact he has spoken so well with his actions through the years adds to his credibility with the kids. Reeves not only bounced back from that career-threatening knee injury, but he also became a cornerstone of the rejuvenation of the Aggies under Jackie Sherrill. Reeves, who lettered from 1981-84, jokes that A&M actually began winning championships in '85 when they dropped the "dead wood." But the influence of '84 seniors like Reeves helped pave the way to Sherrill's magical run. And Reeves, who was originally recruited as a defensive end, paved impressive paths for running backs such as Thomas Sanders, Roger Vick and Anthony Toney.

Reeves was a physically dominating offensive lineman at A&M and was selected as a sixth-round draft pick by the Philadelphia Eagles in '85. He played five seasons in Philly and two more with Cleveland before tearing a biceps muscle and retiring in 1992. After fulfilling his NFL dreams, Reeves returned to A&M to complete unfinished business.

"I lacked two semesters to get my degree in industrial distribution, and when I was in the middle of my first semester I decided that may not be the direction I wanted to go into long term," Reeves said. "I was too far down the road to go back and change my degree plan, so I finished that degree and decided to go to graduate school. I started looking around for different graduate programs and really became interested in the human resources program. I got my master's in human resources training and development while working in human resources for the Department of Food Services on campus. And while I was doing my graduate degree, I was also working in Cain Hall."

Ken Reeves is now an account executive for Countrywide Financial Services in Houston. Along with his wife Lysette, he now preaches the value of education to his own son, Kenneth Wayne Reeves II. Ken's own parents stressed education first throughout his childhood. (Photo courtesy of Ken Reeves)

In addition to working two jobs and earning a master's degree, Reeves also met his wife during his return to Texas A&M. Following the completion of his master's program, Reeves began a successful career in human resources that took him to well known companies such as ConAgra, Natural Gas Clearinghouse, Dynergy, Enron and Reliant. While Reeves enjoyed the human resources industry, he decided to move into mortgage services for a variety of reasons. Mostly, though, he says he loves his daily opportunity to help others realize their dreams.

"I loved human resources, and I am not ruling out the possibility of going back to it," Reeves said. "But I wanted to be more of an entrepreneur and have the opportunity to grow a business where your potential and income is not capped. The most rewarding part of this job is seeing the smiles on people's faces when you help them get the house they want or help them consolidate that debt and pay it off while saving money for retirement or their kids' education."

Whether it's business or personal, Reeves's conversations often come back to education. He was once the parishioner of education sermons in his own home. Now he carries that pulpit with him wherever he goes.

ROD
BERNSTINE

Prior to Rod Bernstine's sophomore season at Texas A&M, then-head coach Jackie Sherrill came to his young running back with the news that he was being moved to tight end. It was enough to send Bernstine off the deep end.

"I didn't respond very well at all," Bernstine said from his home in the Denver suburb of Aurora. "I was very disappointed. Very mad, as a matter of fact."

At the time, Bernstine thought he could forgive Sherrill. Now, as he looks back on his outstanding collegiate and professional career, Bernstine says he can't thank his former coach enough. At A&M, Bernstine went from unwilling tight end in 1984 to first-team All-Southwest Conference by '86. And he is still the most productive pass-catching tight end in Texas A&M history, setting the school record for receptions in one season with 65 in 1986. He also still ranks among the top five in school history with 105 career receptions.

Bernstine then became a first-round draft pick of the San Diego Chargers in 1987, where he played both tight end and running back for six seasons before signing a free agent contract with the Broncos in 1993 and finishing his career in Denver in 1995. Overall, he played nine years

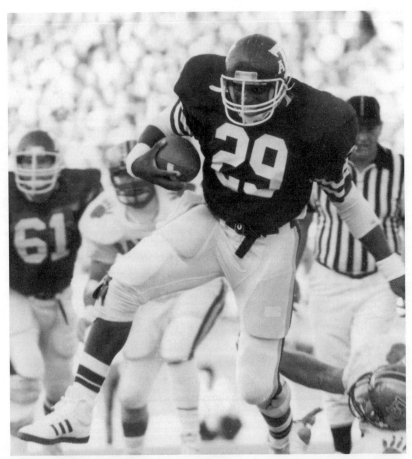

Photo courtesy of Texas A&M Athletic Media Relations

ROD BERNSTINE
A&M Letterman: 1983-86

Position: Tight End, Running Back
All-SWC tight end: 1986
Set A&M's single-season receptions record with 65 in 1986
First-round draft pick of the San Diego Chargers 1987

in the NFL, earning a reputation as one of the more versatile performers in the league.

"In hindsight, things definitely worked out for the best," said Bernstine. "And Jackie never lets me forget that. I still talk to him every once in a while, and he often reminds me how that was the right move for my career. He's right. I got tougher having to block on linebackers and defensive ends, and I was a first-round draft pick. I guess it's funny how things have a way of working out for the best."

For the most part, things have worked out for Bernstine's best interest throughout his life. And whether it was on the field or off, Bernstine has always had a knack for making the most of moves. As a young boy, he grew up in a rough, crime-ridden neighborhood just outside San Francisco. Despite the difficult surroundings, a 14-year-old Bernstine certainly wasn't thrilled by his mother's announcement that she was moving the family from the Bay City to some tiny Texas town by the name of Bryan. But while Bernstine was initially disappointed about leaving the Golden Gate Bridge behind, he soon discovered a golden opportunity awaiting in Brazos County.

"Coming from the San Francisco area, Bryan was a bit of a culture shock for me," Bernstine said. "At first, I thought that was going to be a bad thing. But it turned out to be great for me and my career. When I got to Bryan, I was amazed at how they would basically shut down the town on Friday nights to come watch high school football."

The opportunity to watch Bernstine at the high school level was worth the financial risk of closing shop early. At Bryan High School in the early 1980s, Bernstine was a dynamic, powerful running back, piling up huge rushing totals throughout his career. Even a broken leg he suffered as a junior didn't prevent Bernstine from becoming a preseason all-state selection and a member of the [*Dave Campbell's Texas Football*] Super Team prior to his senior season.

Following his stellar season, Bernstine considered returning to the West, visiting Colorado and USC during the recruiting period. But Bernstine, along with some other local products, believed that the opportunity to be a part of Jackie Sherrill's first recruiting class was too compelling to pass up.

"Going to high school there in Bryan, I saw the struggles A&M had gone through with Tom Wilson there and saw what a commitment the university was making to the football program by hiring Jackie," Bernstine recalled. "I got the feeling that Jackie could turn it around and get things back on track, and I wanted to be a part of that. It didn't happen right away, but that's what happened."

Bernstine played a huge role in making it happen. Bernstine and prolific passer Kevin Murray made more connections in 1985 and '86 than some airlines. The former running back also made things happen after the catch, taking short tosses and turning them into big gains. The '85 Aggies won the school's first outright Southwest Conference title since 1967 and then became the first A&M team since the early 1940s to win back-to-back titles in '86.

"I still take pride in the fact that we were the group that helped establish A&M as a powerful team in the nation," Bernstine said. "It was a very exciting time. While the Aggies have had a few disappointing seasons since I left, the momentum and the championship tradition that we got started has continued to carry on. When I first came to A&M, we weren't even on the national radar. Even when the Aggies have a down season or two, that's no longer the case."

Bernstine made the national radar in the NFL before a torn ACL in 1995—another in a long line of career leg and knee injuries—eventually convinced him it was time to leave the game. After retirement, Bernstine first opened a successful nutritional supplements store and then sold the business in 2000. Since selling the business, he has opened a small stock market investing company from his home, trading stocks for a handful of clients and friends.

While Bernstine devotes plenty of time to his investments, he says his full-time profession might best be described as "Mr. Carpool." Bernstine's wife, Stephanie, owns and operates a take-out pizza company in the Denver area, which means that Bernstine is often charged with delivering his two children to school and practices. His 12-year-old daughter, Payton, is a gymnast and basketball player, while his 10-year-old son, Roderick, is a basketball and football standout.

"I am more or less the stay-at-home dad," Bernstine said. "I can do my investing from home, so I pick up the kids from school and take them to their different sporting events and school functions. I really enjoy it, and I certainly enjoy watching them. They are both athletes. I coach my son's basketball and football teams, so I stay actively involved in their sporting events. Of course, I am a biased, proud dad, but they are both very good athletes and good kids. My son already has some moves on the basketball court and on the football field that make Dad a little envious."

Fortunately for A&M fans, Bernstine says he and his wife, who began dating while they were students at A&M, are raising their children in the Rocky Mountains with an appreciation for Aggieland. Roderick

Rod Bernstine finished his NFL career in Denver and still resides in the Rocky Mountains. Bernstine's wife, Stephanie, owns and operates a take-out pizza company, which means Bernstine is often the carpool king for his daughter Payton and son Roderick. (**Photo courtesy of Rod Bernstine**)

attended the 2003 A&M-Pittsburgh game in College Station and was back for an Aggie football camp in the summer of 2004.

"They are both very aware of Texas A&M and have their fair share of A&M hats, jerseys, T-shirts and so forth," Bernstine said. "My wife and I have so many great memories of our time at Texas A&M, and it's really fun sharing some of those memories with our kids. I'm not sure what they will want to do when that time comes, but if they decided they wanted to go to A&M, I would certainly approve."

And who knows? Perhaps Roderick Bernstine may have the moves to follow in the footsteps of his father, whose reluctant move once helped to reshape the future of Texas A&M's program.

KIP
CORRINGTON

The 2003 press release announcing that Kip Corrington was inducted into the prestigious Verizon Academic All-America Hall of Fame pointed out that the former Texas A&M free safety earned only one "B" throughout his entire four-year career as an undergraduate student.

Big deal, huh? Plenty of average Joes, jocks and marginal students can probably make that same claim. Of course, what separates Kip Corrington from much of the rest of the population is that he was actually disappointed about that lone B. The rest of his transcript was filled with nothing but As.

"Kip was always brilliant, but he never made anybody feel like he was smarter than everybody else," said Corrington's former teammate, Kevin Murray. "Kip was a class act, and it doesn't surprise me one bit to hear how well he is doing now."

Dr. Kip Corrington is certainly doing quite well these days. Corrington, who graduated with his first degree from Texas A&M in 1987 with a 3.98 GPA, is now a specialist in family practice in Greensboro, N.C., where he is employed by Urgent Medical and Family Care. He is a member of the American Academy of Family Practice and the North Carolina Medical Association, and he's had papers published

Photo courtesy of Texas A&M Athletic Media Relations

KIP CORRINGTON
A&M Letterman: 1984-87

Position: Defensive Back
Two-time All-SWC safety: 1986 and '87
Three-time academic All-American: 1985, '86, '87
1987 National Academic All-American of the Year
Captain for the Denver Broncos in Super Bowl XXIV

in numerous outlets, including the *Journal of the American Board of Family Practice*.

In other words, that lone B hasn't continued to haunt him.

"I never really set out to be a doctor," said Corrington, a first-team All-Southwest Conference selection in 1986 and '87 and the only three-time Academic All-American in the history of Texas A&M football. "I was actually planning on being a professor at a college, and I kind of went along that path after I finished playing football. But I eventually decided medicine was a better fit for me because the kind of research I was doing in school didn't allow a lot of contact with people. I like medicine because you can combine the intellectual, scientific part of it with a lot of interaction with people. I'm a people person, and I like working with people."

Corrington regularly helped to work the people inside Kyle Field into a frenzy during his playing days at A&M (1984-87). He weighed only 175 pounds and could have easily been mistaken for a punter or a kicker with his No. 10 jersey hanging loosely from a pair of relatively small shoulder pads.

But Corrington was fearless and always seemed to be around the football, diving into piles, breaking up passes and plowing head-first into running backs who often outweighed him by at least 50 pounds. "I had to be aggressive," Corrington said with a laugh. "As you may recall, I was a little on the small side."

Small frame, yes. But Corrington had a heart as big as Bo Jackson's thighs, which explains how Corrington was able to help corral Jackson in A&M's victory over Auburn in the Cotton Bowl on January 1, 1986. The Aggies' goal-line stand early in the fourth quarter of that Cotton Bowl turned the game around and turned out to be one of the most memorable moments in A&M's history. Jackson was given the ball four consecutive times inside the A&M 6, and each time, the Wrecking Crew turned the Heisman Trophy winner away.

"The goal-line stand was a great moment, and overall, it was a great game to cap a very memorable season," said Corrington, who made an assisted tackle on Jackson's first-down carry. "All three championship seasons were a lot of fun. But that first season and that first Cotton Bowl were probably the most fun, because nobody had expected us to be there. Jackie Sherrill believed strongly in chemistry, and it all came together that year. There was such cohesiveness, and as the year went on, we continued to gain more and more confidence. I'd say that was my favorite year and my favorite Cotton Bowl. It put Texas A&M back on the national spotlight."

The Cotton Bowl appearance was the Aggies' first in 18 years. But A&M may have been waiting at least another year if it not for Corrington's key stop against Arkansas earlier in the year. A&M entered its home showdown against the Hogs with a 6-2 record overall and 4-1 conference mark, while the Razorbacks were 8-1 and ranked in the top 10.

Before an ESPN national television audience, the Aggies built a 10-0 lead in the fourth quarter before the Razorbacks finally mounted a drive deep into A&M territory. Then on fourth and two, Arkansas elected to go for it from the Aggies' 22. Corrington stepped up big-time, producing one of the biggest defensive plays of the year as he stopped burly Arkansas fullback Bobby Joe Edmonds in his tracks. Edmonds was dropped for a one-yard gain, and the Aggies held on for a 10-6 win.

"Personally, that play against Arkansas is my favorite memory," said Corrington, who finished his career with the fifth most interceptions [11] in school history. "We needed a stop, and I managed to take that guy down. But from a team standpoint, I guess my favorite memory is the Texas game [two weeks later]. The crowd was so into that game. I'll never forget it. You could just sense something special in the air. There was no way we were going to lose that game."

The Aggies won the game, 42-10, and went on to win three consecutive SWC titles with Corrington patrolling the secondary. But despite his small stature, Corrington wasn't finished with football after completing his eligibility at A&M. He was drafted by the Detroit Lions in the ninth round of the 1988 draft and spent the next three seasons with the Denver Broncos. Corrington was part of the 1989 AFC championship team in Denver, serving as team captain for Super Bowl XXIV.

After leaving Denver, Corrington moved his family back to College Station, where he began graduate school and later decided to enter medical school. He earned MS, Ph.D. and MD degrees from Texas A&M and formally entered the medical profession in 1999. Now, the man who once showed such complete disregard for his own body is devoted to helping others take care of theirs.

"It is something I enjoy, and it is certainly a challenge," Corrington said. "I do a combination of urgent care. That means everything from dealing with fractures and lacerations to people coming in with the flu. We also take care of people who have had a heart attack or may be coming in with heart failure. It is like a mini-emergency room. We also schedule appointments on certain days just like a traditional family practice."

Kip Corrington, who graduated with his first degree from Texas A&M in 1987 with a 3.98 GPA, is now a specialist in family practice in Greensboro, N.C. His own family includes (from left) daughter Calyste, son Chase, wife Pam, daughter Tana and daughter Kendal. (Photo courtesy of Kip Corrington)

Corrington receives plenty of "family practice" at home, as well. He is the father of four children ranging in ages from eight to 16. And while he was an incredible student, a tremendous football player and is now a highly respected doctor, perhaps the ultimate compliment comes from his wife.

"He was a very good football player throughout his career and is a great doctor," said Corrington's wife, Pam, who was his high school sweetheart at A&M Consolidated High School. "But he's an even better father."

Corrington is such a good father that he's not even afraid to admit his own mistakes to his children. He's even told them about that "B."

RICHMOND WEBB

A dorned in a T-shirt that could fit many mattress sizes and shorts that feature more denim than a cowboy's closet, Richmond Webb strolls through a crowded Houston-area restaurant, causing about as many double-takes as Janet Jackson's halftime shows. At six foot six and in the neighborhood of 365 pounds, Webb is a mountain of a man who stands out in any type of crowd.

Webb wears 38-inch sleeves. Think about that, folks. The average six-foot man typically wears pants that are only 36 inches in length. When Webb spreads out his arms, it creates a wingspan that often registers on the Federal Aviation Administration radar systems. He can grip a basketball like most of the world picks up an orange and casts a shadow that can cause temperature changes. When Webb walks into a room, you get the big picture, and the soft-spoken, mild-mannered Webb receives plenty of stares as people inevitably wonder: "What team did he play for?"

The irony of all the attention Webb usually receives in public is that, for the most part, Webb made quite a comfortable living by blending into the crowd. In 13 NFL seasons, Webb toiled in relative anonymity, as he was rarely in the spotlight, was often overlooked by the media and fans and was almost never singled out by the officials. In fact, about

Photo courtesy of Texas A&M Athletic Media Relations

RICHMOND WEBB
A&M Letterman: 1986-89

Position: Offensive Lineman
First-team All-SWC offensive lineman in 1989
1989 Aggie Heart Award winner
First-round draft pick of the Miami Dolphins in 1990
Seven-time Pro Bowl selection

the only time that Webb was consistently mentioned during his pro football career was around Pro Bowl time. In that realm, Webb owns a distinction like no other Miami Dolphins player.

Dan Marino didn't do it. Larry Csonka can't make the same claim, either. Neither can Garo Yepremian, Bob Griese, Paul Warfield, Nick Buoniconti or any of the other legendary players in the history of the Dolphins. The only player in the history of the franchise who has ever been selected to the Pro Bowl in each of his first seven seasons in the league is Richmond Webb.

That remarkable string of consistency helped Webb, at the peak of his career, to become one of the highest-paid offensive linemen in NFL history. Overall, he played 13 seasons in the NFL, starting in 183 of the 184 games he played. During his 11 years with the Dolphins, Webb helped Miami make the playoffs eight times. He then finished his career with two more seasons in Cincinnati.

Those are the kinds of numbers and honors that could eventually earn Webb a call from Canton, Ohio, home of the Pro Football Hall of Fame. The unassuming Webb practically blushes at the mere mention of the Hall of Fame, but he does acknowledge that his extraordinary longevity on the offensive line was "not bad" for a guy who never even figured he would play that position. Webb came to Texas A&M with the intention of terrorizing quarterbacks, not protecting them.

"I never dreamed things would work out this way, first of all because I was a defensive lineman coming out of Dallas Roosevelt High School," Webb said from his home in the Houston area. "I was recruited for defense, and I played defense my first year before they moved me to offense where I was backing up Louis Cheek. I learned a lot from Louis and other guys on the offensive line like Jerry Fontenot. And then Joe Avezzano, who went on to become the special teams coach for the Dallas Cowboys, was the offensive line coach. He taught me a lot. But even with such great teaching, in no way, shape or form did I expect to be a first-round draft pick in the NFL. It caught me by surprise. Basically, I was going to school to get an education and playing football for a university that I really loved. The NFL never really crossed my mind at the start of my college career. I was just trying to do my best."

By the time he finished his collegiate career in 1989, however, Webb was viewed as one of the nation's best. After helping the Aggies to three bowl games, two conference titles and an overall record of 34-14 from 1986-89, Webb earned first-team All-Southwest Conference and second-team All-America honors as a senior. And then the young man who once had no pro expectations was selected in the first round of the

1990 NFL draft with the ninth overall pick. He was the only offensive lineman selected in the first round.

NFL scouts drooled when they assessed Webb's potential; NFL coaches coveted his quick feet and extraordinary reach. And the Dolphins believed Webb was the perfect watchdog to protect their most valuable commodity: Marino.

"His body is a gift," former A&M offensive line coach and current Green Bay Packers head coach Mike Sherman once said about Webb. "You couldn't ask for a more perfect physical package for a left tackle. The good Lord blessed him with extremely long arms, and if Richmond makes a mistake with his feet, those long arms can help him recover and keep from getting beat on a play. Left tackle is the position Richmond was born to play."

It was also a position Webb was once reluctant to play. Webb arrived at A&M in 1985, tipping the scales at a lean 240 pounds. Following a redshirt season in '85, he made the switch from defense to offense, where he was a starter at left guard during his sophomore and junior seasons. But in the spring drills of 1989, A&M coaches began pondering another move for Webb because the Aggie offense couldn't seem to control Webb's former high school teammate, Aaron Wallace.

"Aaron was a real thorn in the side of our offense," recalled Webb, the 1989 winner of the prestigious Aggie Heart Award. "He was a great player and obviously was an outstanding pass rusher. So they moved me over to tackle to block against Aaron. I wasn't really happy about the move at first because I was comfortable at guard. But I adapted, and it really helped me to go against a player of Aaron's quality."

Wallace helped Webb to prepare for the Bruce Smiths, Derrick Thomases and Lawrence Taylors of the NFL. And as the 1990 season began, Webb became only the third offensive rookie in Dolphins history to start in the season opener, joining Otto Stowe and Larry Csonka on that distinguished, short list.

Right from the start, it was apparent that Webb was destined for greatness. In his rookie season, he allowed just two sacks and was penalized for holding just once all season. In three games against Buffalo's Smith, who was the 1990 NFL Defensive Player of the Year, Webb allowed no sacks. And in 12 quarters lined up against Webb, Smith accounted for only seven tackles. He was simply amazing as a rookie, and he was even better as he developed over the next few seasons.

"My job was to keep Dan Marino's uniform clean," Webb said. "That was my sole purpose, and if Dan looked good, I was doing my job. Everybody in Miami loved Dan, and when I first got to Miami, I was

When he chose Texas A&M over Oklahoma and Oklahoma State as his collegiate destination, Richmond Webb vowed to his mother, Bobbie, that he would earn his degree. In each of his first three NFL off seasons, he returned to A&M to go back to school. In 1993, he graduated with a degree in industrial distribution. (Photo courtesy of Texas A&M Athletic Media Relations)

scared to death of someday being the guy that allowed Marino to get hurt. So my motivation initially was more out of fear than anything else. But as time went by, I became more of a student of the game and learned to rely on my knowledge of the game as much as my physical abilities."

Whether it was football or anything else, Webb was always the studious type. He was the class president at Roosevelt High School and an outstanding student. When he chose Texas A&M over Oklahoma and Oklahoma State as his collegiate destination, Webb vowed to his mother, Bobbie Webb, that he would earn his degree. In each of his first three NFL off seasons, he returned to A&M to go back to school, and in 1993, he graduated with a degree in industrial distribution.

"I remember when I came back the first time and just going back to classes with some of the guys," said Webb, who celebrated his 37th birthday in January of 2004. "They would all ask, 'If you're making all this money now, why are you coming back?' But that was the main thing I went to A&M for—to earn a degree. I was blessed to get a scholarship from A&M, and I always wanted to get a degree because of the strong alumni association and just the prestige of the degree. A&M is one of the schools that is respected not only in the state of Texas, but in the United States. The feeling of going across the stage to get my degree is hard to describe. But I advise all athletes to go back and get that. If they don't get it while they're playing, go back and get it."

Throughout his 13-year NFL career, Webb consistently used his mind as much as his body. He began investing much of his salary early in his pro career, as he always kept in mind that his career could end with an injury at any moment. When the career-ending injury finally occurred—a torn pectoral muscle four games into the 2002 season— Webb rivaled the FDIC in terms of financial security. And in 2003—his first season out of the game in more than a quarter of a century—Webb was struck by the realization of how little he actually missed the game.

"I did miss the camaraderie of my teammates and just hanging out with the guys in the locker room," said Webb, who has three daughters, 16-year-old Jasmine, seven-year-old Brianna and two-year-old Madison. "But I didn't miss training camp, and I kind of enjoyed sitting back on the couch and watching the games with my family. I'm not sure how much my wife enjoyed me being around all the time, but I think she's getting used to it now."

Webb met his wife, Chandra, at Texas A&M, and they both have several business ventures on the front burner. Chandra is involved in a home-based business, making baskets and natural stone jewelry. Richmond partnered with another former A&M star, Aaron Glenn, in a commercial real estate venture in Sugarland. Webb says the strip center project allowed him to get his feet wet in commercial real estate development, and he says it is something he plans to continue doing in the future.

Webb also has a business partner who trains the cutting horses that Webb owns on his sprawling, 100-acre property in Schulenburg, which is located along Interstate 10 between Houston and San Antonio. Overall, Webb owns a dozen cutting horses and about 40 head of cattle. Webb doesn't participate in any of the training, but he does enjoy an occasional horseback ride.

"Most of all, I like to get on the land and ride my four-wheeler," Webb said. "But I will take a horse out for a walk. I'm not on the verge of becoming the next Roy Rogers or training for the rodeo, but we like getting out on the land and just enjoying a little country atmosphere. It's relaxing, and it kind of allows us to escape from the hustle and bustle of the crowds. I'll always be grateful for the opportunities Texas A&M and the NFL provided me, but I'm really enjoying this next stage of my life."

Indeed, the man with 38-inch sleeves has "reached" an enjoyable stage called the "good life." You'd probably expect nothing less from the gentle giant who has always stood out in the crowd and been a standout in front of the crowds.

WARREN BARHORST

Alex Morris had a key interception to turn the momentum in Texas A&M's favor. Darren Lewis completed a halfback pass for the game-tying touchdown. Bucky Richardson rushed for 96 yards and two touchdowns and was voted the game's Most Valuable Player.

Obviously, there were plenty of key contributors to Texas A&M's 35-10 win over Notre Dame in the 1988 Cotton Bowl—a victory that easily ranks as one of the most impressive bowl triumphs in school history. But perhaps the most memorable and lasting moment from that game was turned in by a walk-on who once figured he wasn't cut out for college football. Not even at Stephen F. Austin State University.

12th Man Kickoff Team member Warren Barhorst endeared himself to Aggies everywhere and enraged Heisman Trophy winner Tim Brown when Barhorst first wrapped up the Notre Dame superstar and then ripped off his belt towel. Infuriated, Brown raced toward the A&M sideline and jumped on Barhorst's back. That series of events earned Barhorst a place in A&M history and earned Brown a 15-yard penalty and an ejection from the game. Although it happened more than 15 years ago, many Aggies have not forgotten. In a survey conducted by the Texas A&M Letterman's Association, Barhorst's thievery was voted as the fifth most memorable moment in Aggie history. And Barhorst, now the

Photo courtesy of Texas A&M Athletic Media Relations

WARREN BARHORST
A&M Letterman: 1987

Position: 12th Man Kickoff Team Member in 1987

owner of a successful insurance agency chain, says people constantly want to talk about it.

"On average, I probably talk about it five times a week," said Barhorst, who resides in Houston with his wife, Lisa, and three children. "Friends, colleagues, clients, strangers—you name it—bring it up."

The fact that he has been remembered—let alone revered—for so long strikes Barhorst as humorous and remarkably ironic. First of all, Barhorst didn't plan on playing college football. Secondly, he began his collegiate career at Stephen F. Austin. And finally, it wasn't even his idea to steal Brown's towel.

"It's pretty strange how things work out," said Barhorst, who earned his degree in industrial distribution in 1988. "I have three brothers and sisters that all went to A&M before me, but I guess I was a weenie and ended up starting out at SFA. I didn't even play football there. Coming out of high school, I weighed about 180 pounds and figured I was too small and beat up to play. But then I went from 180 to 210 pounds my freshman year in college, and I transferred to A&M after two years because my brother, Alan, had come back to work on his master's in mechanical engineering. I decided to try out for the 12th Man Kickoff Team, and the rest is history."

Barhorst, who played fullback and linebacker at Jersey Village High School in the Houston area, answered an advertisement in the school newspaper and was among the estimated 350 walk,ons who tried out for the 12th Man Kickoff Team in 1986. He made the squad, but was unable to participate in any games because of his transfer. When he was told he would not be able to play that first year, Barhorst nearly hung up his cleats for good. But several other members of the 12th Man Kickoff Team talked him into hanging around. And in 1987, Barhorst, who bulked up to 225 pounds, was a key contributor on the kickoff team, which then featured 10 walk-ons and a scholarship kicker (Scott Slater).

As A&M rolled toward its third consecutive Southwest Conference title, Barhorst and the wild bunch on the 12th Man Kickoff Team continued to attract national attention to Texas A&M. The concept Jackie Sherrill had introduced was now a national headliner, and one of the interesting angles of the 1988 Cotton Bowl was the matchup between the 12th Man Kickoff Team and the Heisman Trophy winner. Brown, who went on to become the Oakland Raiders' all-time leading receiver, established a Notre Dame school record for the most career kickoff return yards. It's a record that still stands and one that provided plenty of motivation for the Aggies' kickoff unit.

"We certainly didn't want to let him beat us," Barhorst said. "We looked at it as a real challenge to keep him under control."

The idea to take Brown's towel, however, did not come from Barhorst or any other members of the 12th Man Kickoff Team. That notion was planted by defensive back Chet Brooks, who is also credited with pinning the "Wrecking Crew" nickname on the A&M defense. Brooks had played high school football against Brown in the Dallas area. According to Barhorst, Brooks didn't hold Brown in the highest regard, but he did have some insight into Brown's pet peeves.

"They had played each other in high school, and [Brooks] told the guys on the 12th Man Kickoff Team to steal his towel," Barhorst said. "Chet said that would drive him crazy."

Brooks was right. After A&M had taken a 28-10 lead in the fourth quarter, Barhorst got the best of Brown. Twice.

"If you watch the film of that thing, I almost got beat," Barhorst said. "He's two steps away from going for six. But I made the tackle on him and acted on Chet's idea. Those guys had been stealing our towels all day, and I swiped it and started running off the field while trying to stuff the towel in my pants. I was pretty shocked when Brown jumped on my back. I guess he got the towel back. I have always assumed the towel fell out and Brown picked it up. Maybe you should ask him. He might want to clear his name."

Brown was ejected, and Barhorst instantly became a legend in Aggie lore, although it took some time for the TV announcers to correctly identify him. Barhorst, who wore No. 11, was first identified by the CBS broadcast crew as redshirt freshman William Thomas, who went on to NFL stardom. But Aggies who identified with the walk-ons of the 12th Man Kickoff Team quickly learned the name Warren Barhorst. In fact, Barhorst was even prominently featured in a limited edition painting that hangs in his office today.

"My wife and I got married my senior year in school and we were poorer than churchmice," Barhorst said. "Jackie Sherrill called me and asked if I had seen this painting. I called the artist and found out that he was only going to do 150 copies and he wanted $500 for it. I didn't have $500, so my sister who is a big Aggie and in the Class of '79 bought it for me."

Today, the Barhorsts are no longer poorer than churchmice. After graduation, Barhorst initially sold industrial equipment and then went into the insurance business in 1993. Since opening his first Nationwide Insurance storefront in Houston, Barhorst has opened two other locations in Houston and added stores in Abilene, Amarillo, Baytown, El

From left, Spencer, Shelby, Lisa, Warren and Ashley Barhorst ham it up for the photographer near their Houston-area home. Warren Barhorst met his wife Lisa while he was attending Texas A&M, and he jokingly says he stalked her long enough that she finally consented to a date. The former walk-on now operates a thriving insurance agency. (Photo courtesy of Warren Barhorst)

Paso and Tomball. Overall, he has eight locations, and out of 4,700 Nationwide stores across the country, Barhorst's businesses ranked in the top 10 nationally.

"I never did dream of this when I started off," said Barhorst, the father of three children ranging in ages from eight to 17. "I thought if I had three or four employees that would be great. But you start making your goals and writing them down, planning and pushing, and goals seem to come true. I am real competitive, and I will say that my experiences at A&M have really helped me in business. Being a walk-on teaches you how to face long odds and being on that kickoff team certainly taught me how to perform under pressure. Plus, I have surrounded myself with good people and hired a great team to operate stores. We've been very fortunate, but we've also put in the work."

Barhorst has also been generous with his success. He was one of the first former players to contribute financially to the players' lounge in the new Bright Football Complex, which opened in the south end zone of Kyle Field in 2003. The players' lounge was funded entirely by donations from former players, and Barhorst says it was a privilege to pay his alma mater back.

"It's an honor to be able to give back to the program," Barhorst said. "I learned a lot and had so much fun being a part of that 12th Man Kickoff Team. I just never figured that people would still remember me."

On average, he receives about five reminders per week that they do still remember. The once-anonymous walk-on has seen his 15 minutes of fame last for more than 15 years, with no foreseeable end in sight.

MIKE
ARTHUR

During his six-year NFL career with the Cincinnati Bengals, New England Patriots and Green Bay Packers, Mike Arthur may have witnessed more teammates making significant mistakes with their checkbooks than their playbooks. Guys who made brilliant decisions and incredible moves on the field would often go brain-dead with their finances.

"It was pretty amazing to see these college kids come into the NFL and go from nothing to having a ton of money," said Arthur, who now resides with his family in Cincinnati. "But it's also really sad to see how many of those guys blow their money. Some of them get taken advantage of when they get into the NFL by people around them giving them bad advice. Others get up there, look at the guy they're playing next to who is making $1 or $2 million a year and try to keep up with the Joneses. That's how some of the guys leave the NFL in debt or in a difficult financial situation, even though they've been making a very good salary. It's a sad situation that happens to far too many players."

It's an easy trap for young players to fall into in the extravagant world of monstrous salaries, enormous signing bonuses and gigantic egos. But for Arthur, it was also a relatively easy pitfall to avoid. Arthur entered the NFL with an interest in investing, and as he watched others

Photo courtesy of the Texas A&M Athletic Sports Museum

MIKE ARTHUR
A&M Letterman: 1987-90

Position: Offensive Lineman
First-team All-SWC center in 1990
First-team All-America center in 1990
Fifth-round draft pick of the Cincinnati Bengals in 1991

around him spend like there was no tomorrow, he developed a passion for planning for the future.

In the process, Arthur established a firm financial situation for himself and also found a full-time occupation in his post-NFL career. Today, the well-spoken, unassuming Arthur is a financial planner with Smith Barney. While he has numerous clients from different walks of life and various professions, Arthur is particularly passionate about reaching out to young NFL players.

"I got into investing and financial planning when I was making some money in the NFL," Arthur said. "I started investing on my own and really enjoyed it. I got a kick out of coming home and reading and learning about it. It turned into my hobby. Then when I finished playing, I decided this was the perfect line of work for me. I enjoy helping people with their investing and retirement plans, and I take a particular interest in trying to help some of these young guys coming into the league to avoid the financial downfalls that others have gone through. I make it a point to tell them that once football is over, the chances of immediately making that much money in a traditional business field aren't real good. I also tell them that this is a once-in-a-lifetime opportunity that isn't going to last long. They hear that a lot, but I am the perfect example that the NFL is a here-today, gone-tomorrow business."

Arthur has the scars to prove it. After his brilliant career at A&M ended in 1990 with first-team All-America honors, the power-blocking center was a fifth-round draft pick of the Bengals. Arthur spent his first three NFL seasons in Cincinnati, where he also met his wife, Susan. He then played two years with the New England Patriots and joined the Packers in 1995. It was in Green Bay that Arthur's football career came grinding to a halt.

He suffered a serious knee injury in the 1996 preseason and was released by Green Bay at the end of November—less than two months before the Packers would go on to win the Super Bowl. In another reminder of just how cruel the NFL can be, Arthur wasn't even awarded a Super Bowl ring.

"Not getting to go to the Super Bowl and not getting a chance to earn that ring was a little disappointing because I was so close," Arthur said. "But on the other hand, I really never expected to even get a chance to play pro football. So I look back on the time that I did have as a tremendous blessing. I enjoyed it, and I also met some people who had a major, positive influence on my life. It's all a matter of perspective, and I try to dwell on the positives."

When he looks back at his time in the NFL, Arthur chooses not to focus on how a knee injury limited his ability to run, but rather on how his time in professional football improved his Christian walk. As a wide-eyed rookie with the Bengals in 1991, Arthur played alongside Hall of Famer Anthony Munoz, a devout Christian and devoted family man who served as a role model to Arthur both on and off the field. Then with the Packers, Arthur was a teammate of another Hall of Famer, Reggie White, who is a minister and outspoken proponent of conservative Christian values.

"Playing with guys like that and growing spiritually stronger because of their witness was far more valuable than any number of Super Bowl rings would be," Arthur said. "God has definitely blessed me and my family in so many ways, and I give all glory to Him. Some of the guys I played with helped my wife and me so much in terms of our relationship with Christ that I want to do the same for others. I've had some wonderful mentors, and I'd like to live my life in a manner that could serve as an example to others, especially my children."

Arthur is a devoted family man and a doting father of three—nine-year-old daughter Allison, seven-year-old son Nicholas and three-year-old son Nathan. It was primarily because of his family that Arthur chose in 2003 to leave Houston for Cincinnati. He first fell in love with the Midwest while he was playing with the Bengals, and he and his wife had been considering a permanent return for some time.

"My wife was raised in Cincinnati, and I really liked the city when I was playing," said Arthur, who was raised in Houston and attended Spring Woods High School. "It is just a nice Midwestern city and a great place to raise a family. I've spent most of my life in Texas, and I still love Texas. But this was a positive move for us. Of course, we're a long way from Texas A&M, but I can still follow the Aggies and teach my kids all about A&M. And we'll still come back from time to time."

The entire Arthur clan was in attendance in 2003 when Arthur received what he calls his greatest honor in football—being inducted into the Texas A&M Athletic Hall of Fame. Arthur had spent some of his youth dreaming about playing for the Aggies after watching his oldest brother, Bob, attend A&M and his middle brother, Tom, serve as a captain of the 12th Man Kickoff Team when that tradition was first introduced by Jackie Sherrill in 1983.

So when the opportunity to play for the Aggies arose, Arthur leapt at it. After being redshirted in the Aggies' 1986 SWC title season, Arthur earned his first significant playing time in A&M's 35-10 victory over Notre Dame in the 1988 Cotton Bowl. Then he made his first start in

Mike Arthur and his wife, Susan, left Houston in 2003 to reside in Cincinnati, where the couple met, with their children (from left) Nicholas, Allison and Nathan. Arthur is a successful financial planner who has worked with many current and former NFL players. (Photo courtesy of the Texas A&M Athletic Sports Museum)

the Kickoff Classic against Nebraska in Sherrill's final season. His collegiate career ended in memorable fashion, as well. The Aggies thoroughly whipped BYU, 65-14, in the Holiday Bowl and established the record for most points scored in a bowl game.

"That was definitely a great way to go out," Arthur said. "But overall, I'd say my entire career at A&M was very rewarding, and it was a tremendous honor to get into the A&M Hall of Fame. I wasn't expecting it, and when I first got the phone call, I thought it was someone playing a joke on me. But it was a very big honor for my family and me to be recognized that way. It is something that I will always cherish. You can't put a price tag on something like that."

If you could, you can be assured that Arthur would thoroughly investigate before buying in. He doesn't just talk the talk of financial responsibility; he also walks the walk.

JOHN
ELLISOR

L ike so many other Texas A&M football players through the years, John Ellisor grew up dreaming of making a name for himself at Kyle Field. Ellisor's childhood vision, however, involved standing on the east sidelines of the triple-decked stadium and leading his beloved Texas Longhorns to victories against the Aggies.

Raised in Kingwood, Ellisor was once a diehard burnt orange backer, wearing his UT baseball caps, T-shirts, jackets and other authentic gear whenever and wherever he could. He flashed the "hook 'em" hand signal with pride, hummed "Texas Fight" day and night and longed for the day when he would become a Longhorn. Following a stellar prep football career at Kingwood High School, Ellisor received an opportunity to fulfill all of his Austin aspirations.

So what happened to suddenly change the blue-chip prospect's blood from burnt orange to deep maroon? It was actually nothing extraordinary. Ellisor, an All-State offensive lineman at Kingwood, visited Texas, Nebraska, UCLA, Oklahoma and Texas A&M during the winter of 1987-88. He returned home from those recruiting visits and promptly began emptying his orange paraphernalia from the closet. Ellisor suddenly realized he no longer needed burnt orange clothing, because it was A&M that fit him so perfectly.

Photo courtesy of Texas A&M Athletic Media Relations

JOHN ELLISOR
A&M Letterman: 1988-92

Position: Offensive Lineman
First-team All-SWC offensive lineman 1991 and '92
Honorable mention All-America in 1992
Helped '91 team set school scoring record (36.6 points per game)

"Once I met the guys on the team and met the students, I just knew A&M was the right place for me," said Ellisor, who was primarily recruited by A&M assistant Jim Helms. "It was the people. I got up there and met Mike Arthur, Bucky Richardson and a bunch of other guys, and those were just the kind of people I wanted to be around. I couldn't put my finger on what it was exactly, but there was something special about A&M, and I just knew I had to be a part of it."

Ellisor, on the other hand, wasn't necessarily a special player right away. When he arrived on the A&M campus in the summer of 1988, the powerful blocker was moved to the other side of the line of scrimmage. Playing nose guard, Ellisor felt completely out of place. It wasn't a natural transition for him, but Ellisor did make a contribution as a true freshman, recording five tackles for the season.

But before he would truly make an impact, Ellisor would first land in a heap of hot water. During the summer prior to his sophomore season, he suffered a knee injury while sliding into home plate in a slow-pitch softball game.

"Nobody was real happy about that," Ellisor recalled. "So I was redshirted during 1989, and then I was switched back to the offensive line and started playing guard in 1990. It was a really a good move for me, because I felt like I was back where I belonged."

Back in his natural element, Ellisor emerged as a starter at guard by the midway point of the '90 season and played a key role in A&M's assault on the Southwest Conference's rushing records. The 1990 Aggies rushed for a SWC-record 3,829 yards and produced an astonishing 18 100-yard individual rushing performances. Ellisor earned honorable mention All-SWC honors as a sophomore, and in '91, he and the Aggies were even better.

The 1991 Aggies rolled to a 10-1 record in the regular season, claimed the first of three straight SWC titles and scored more points (402) than any other team in school history. Opening holes for talented tailbacks like Greg Hill and Rodney Thomas, Ellisor was selected as a first-team All-SWC performer in both 1991 and '92. The individual honors were nice, Ellisor says. But that was never his goal, and it's not what he remembers most fondly when he looks back.

"It was a great time to be an Aggie football player," said Ellisor, who now resides with his family in Kingwood. "To me, that was just a pinnacle time to be a football player at A&M. We were dominating the Southwest Conference, and we really felt like we were putting A&M on the elite map of college football. I am not one of the guys who can tell you I did this against TCU or such and such happened against Arkansas.

I have friends like that, but for me it is more of a collage of memories that just leave me with a feeling of being a part of something so special. It was nice to be recognized individually, but to this day what I am most proud of is that I can say I am an Aggie. I am part of something that is so great and people have so much respect for and people are so proud to be a part of."

Ellisor is now making certain his own young children understand the uniqueness of Aggieland. His five-year-old daughter, Emily, and three-year-old son, John Lawson, already are well versed in Aggie traditions and lore. And he has complete confidence that his one-year-old son, Jack, will soon be flashing the "Gig 'em" sign long before learning less important things like walking and talking.

"Being a dad is the greatest thing that ever happened to me," said Ellisor, who met his wife, Gretchen, while at A&M. "It's really great to be able to share with them the things that we love, including our love for A&M. We're bringing 'em up the right way, as opposed to the way I grew up loving that other school. They can learn from their daddy's mistakes. And I think my oldest boy has a lot of his father in him. He's a big boy. He's destined to have a 5, 6 or 7 as the first number on his jersey. It would be a bonus if any of my kids get the opportunity to be a student-athlete at A&M, but the main thing is just for them to go to A&M and experience the tradition and the quality of people that attend the university. That is where I have made my lifelong friends, and it is an opportunity I pray they will have the chance to experience. That would be a dream come true for their father."

Ellisor's dreams of a career in the NFL didn't materialize the way he had once envisioned. Wrist injuries while he was at A&M played a major role in NFL teams shying away from him during the 1993 draft, and Ellisor signed as a free agent with the Chicago Bears. During his first training camp with the Bears, Ellisor broke his wrist again, ending his NFL career before it ever really started. Fortunately for Ellisor, an agricultural economics major, he enjoyed another prime option.

His father started his own company, Ellisor Constructors, in 1989. The general contracting company specializes in commercial construction and also encompasses a site-work company. When the NFL didn't pan out, Ellisor went to work with his father.

"Of course, I planned to play in the NFL," Ellisor said. "But it kind of worked out for the best. It was an opportunity that was given to me when I graduated, and I took advantage of it. My specific role is that I estimate and project manage, and I oversee the operations. I enjoy it

John Ellisor now runs Ellisor Constructors in the Houston area. He and his wife, Gretchen, raise a growing family—daughter Emily, son John Lawson, and son Jack (not pictured)—in Kingwood. (Photo courtesy of John Ellisor)

quite a bit. It is kind of different every day, and the thing about this business is you learn something every day."

Ellisor makes it a point to attend at least a few A&M games each year. And no matter how many times he returns, he says he is always overcome with the electricity of a game day in College Station. But when asked if he still has the itch to put on the pads, the quick-witted Ellisor could barely contain his laughter.

"No, those days are behind me," he said. "I absolutely loved playing at A&M and going to school at A&M, and I am so thankful for the opportunities that the school provided me and the doors it opened. But I like to remember myself playing at a real high level, and my memory is probably a lot better now than my reality."

Where Have You Gone?

ANTONIO ARMSTRONG

Sitting on a park swing, seven-year-old Joshua Armstrong listens intently to stories about his father's football exploits and seems genuinely impressed. He nods approvingly when the sacks, the tackles and the honors are described, as his bright eyes widen in authentic astonishment with the specific details of his father's gridiron glory.

"Daddy was pretty great back then, huh?" says Joshua, who is as quick-witted as his compelling father. "I already knew Daddy was awesome, but it's nice to know you agree. Daddy can do anything."

His father, former Texas A&M outside linebacker Antonio Armstrong, has proven he can overcome almost anything. And not just in the eyes of his children. Armstrong, who grew up in Houston without a father, takes tremendous pride in providing the paternal involvement to his children that he never experienced. His kids, Joshua, three-year-old Antonio Jr. and infant daughter Kayra, adore him. The feeling is mutual.

But Armstrong, whose chiseled physique is more impressive today than when he was a wrecking ball on the Wrecking Crew, is more than merely a role model for his offspring. He's the embodiment of courage with charisma, facing abandonment, life-threatening illness, broken limbs, rejection and bankruptcy with a contagious smile.

Photo courtesy of Texas A&M Athletic Media Relations

ANTONIO ARMSTRONG
A&M Letterman: 1991-94

Position: Linebacker
First-team All-America linebacker in 1994
First-team All-SWC linebacker in 1993 and '94
154 career tackles and 18 sacks
Sixth-round draft pick of the San Francisco 49ers in 1995

"He's easy to root for in anything he does," said Mike Clark, A&M's former assistant athletic director for strength and conditioning. "If you can't root for a guy like Antonio, you're probably just evil. His personality, his smile and his attitude are just infectious. And he has overcome so much."

Armstrong, who celebrated his 30th birthday in 2003, has probably tackled more obstacles than ball carriers in his lifetime. He has learned to deal with adversity without being aversely affected. And he has refused to allow nightmares to interfere with his dreams.

A devout Christian, Armstrong quotes Biblical passages with the ease of a minister and is especially quick to recite scriptures dealing with perseverance and enduring tough times. Of course, he could probably write his own book about those subjects.

Armstrong was born to a 15-year-old mother and fathered by a 16-year-old boy. He says his father had good intentions, but he was unequipped, unprepared and unable to provide for a child when he was practically a child himself. His father dropped out of high school to find a job when Antonio was born, and when money became scarce, he turned to the streets.

"The next thing you know, he got involved in drugs and the streets consumed him," Armstrong said of his father. "He passed away the month before I came to Texas A&M, and I never really knew him. That's a big reason why I take being a father to my kids so seriously. It's my purpose in life. I don't want to see my kids struggle like I struggled growing up. My mother didn't have the ability to give me a home like my kids have now."

Armstrong, who is now a personal trainer in Houston and owns a successful health and nutritional supplements distributorship, also has provided his kids with a different name than he had while growing up. Antonio Armstrong was raised as Antonio Shorter, and he spent his first three years at A&M with "SHORTER" on the back of his jersey. But in one of the ultimate testaments of being able to forgive and remember, Shorter changed his last name to Armstrong to honor the father he had never really known. He also dedicated the 1994 season to his father.

It was a memorable season, to say the least. Armstrong was the leader of a defensive unit that finished fourth nationally in scoring defense (13.4 points per game) and fifth in total defense. He was also one of the prominent leaders of a team that completed just the ninth unbeaten season in Texas A&M history (10-0-1) and the first since 1956.

Armstrong recorded 62 tackles in 1994, including 17 behind the line of scrimmage, to earn All-America honors. And his three sacks against Notre Dame in the 1994 Cotton Bowl—going against All-American Aaron Taylor—helped him earn defensive MVP honors in that game.

Of course, the fact that he even played college football could probably be considered miraculous. Without a father figure and without any luxuries to speak of, a young Armstrong found refuge on the football field. Armstrong emerged as a star at Houston's Kashmere High School, but just as he began to rise to new heights, his health sank to the lowest of depths. As a senior at Kashmere, Armstrong was diagnosed with a brain aneurysm, placing both his football future and his life in jeopardy.

"The doctors didn't know if I was going to live or die," Armstrong said. "They said that if I did come out of it, I would never play football again. But thankfully, I had a praying mother, and she wouldn't stop praying. With the aneurysm, I would come in and out of consciousness. Days would pass, and I would not know where I was. They kept me sedated to keep me from having seizures. I didn't eat, and I lost tons of weight. At that time in my life, I knew of God, but I didn't know Christ as my personal savior. But about two or three weeks after I was released from the hospital, the doctors ran a CAT scan and told me I would have scar tissue and would have severe headaches for the rest of my life.

"To make a long story short, I went to a church service and met this man, who asked if anybody had physical ailments. I went up and he prayed for me. I went back to the doctor, and he said there were no traces of scar tissue, and he released me to play football. It was nothing short of a miracle from God."

It was a miraculous recovery, but most of the schools that had shown interest in him before the brain aneurysm—Oklahoma, Texas, Colorado and UCLA, to name a few—no longer wanted him. Only A&M continued to express interest, so Armstrong signed with the Aggies in 1991.

But after losing so much weight, he was in for a rude awakening. Armstrong was so undersized during the early part of his freshman season that the A&M video staff made him the star of a mock "crash dummy" tape, showing footage of tight ends like Greg Schorp, James McKeehan and Jason Matthews driving Armstrong 10 to 20 yards off the line of scrimmage.

"He wasn't even 200 pounds, probably closer to 190, the day he first stepped foot on this campus," Clark said of Armstrong. "He was skinny, and he just got thrown around like a rag doll in practice. But he got in the weight room and got after it right away. He was one of those kids who was always fun to work with and was always willing to work.

Antonio Armstrong and his wife, Dawn, maintain a full house in their
Houston-area home with (from left) Joshua, Kayra and Antonio Jr. Armstrong
was an All-SWC linebacker in 1993 when he went by the last name of "Shorter"
and then won All-America honors in 1994 after changing his last name. (**Photo**
courtesy of Antonio Armstrong)

He was always like, 'OK, Coach, what do you want me to do next?' He
was one heckuva hard worker."

Armstrong, who played primarily on special teams as a freshman,
worked so hard in the off season and increased his strength so dramatically that Clark had him tested for steroids. But Armstrong was as clean
as a "G"-rated movie. He took a summer job moving furniture and practically lived in the weight room. By 1993, Armstrong weighed 225
pounds and was an instant hit in the starting lineup, earning All-SWC
honors with 73 tackles and 8.5 sacks.

He then finished off his A&M career with a sensational senior season in '94, but he had to overcome another debilitating injury to do it.
Prior to his senior year, Armstrong was diagnosed with a rare and painful
condition called osteitis pubis, in which he was constantly tearing his
abdominal muscles from his pelvic bone.

"Even though I made All-American as a senior, I didn't play as well as I could have because of the physical limitations," Armstrong said. "I lost a step or two in my quickness, and it really bothered me. The injury didn't allow me to run for all the scouts, either. I was labeled as 'damaged goods' by the NFL, and that's why I slipped into the sixth round before the San Francisco 49ers took me."

Armstrong literally cried on draft day. But things quickly began working out in San Francisco. With the injury finally behind him, Armstrong played extremely well in training camp and moved to second team on the depth chart. It looked as if the 'Niners had found a steal in the sixth round, but Armstrong then fractured his right leg. And on his 22nd birthday, the 49ers released him.

The Dolphins picked him up the next day, and he spent the rest of the 1995 season in Miami. But after Jimmy Johnson became the head coach of the Dolphins, Armstrong supposedly didn't fit into Johnson's system. Then it was on to St. Louis, where he was later released by the Rams. He sat out the entire 1996 season and then gave the Canadian Football League a shot in '97 at Toronto. The scenario north of the border was basically the same. Armstrong actually made the team, but was released three days into the season. Even for the ever-optimistic Armstrong, it was a devastating blow followed by an all-time low.

"After being released by Toronto, I found myself at the lowest point in my life," Armstrong said. "At first, I was making $10,000 to $12,000 every two weeks, and I was living in the fast lane. I wasn't ever really bad and into hard-core drugs or anything like that, but from a Biblical standpoint, I wasn't living a holy life. Then my cars were repossessed; I lost my home and found myself with absolutely nothing. I was in my mother's house at rock bottom. I can remember it was November 10 or 11 in 1997, and I went to church and gave my life to Christ. I was tired of living the way I was living."

From that point, Armstrong's outlook began to improve. In 1998, Toronto traded his rights to the British Columbia Lions, and he was married to his wife, Dawn, later that same year. Armstrong and his wife figured the CFL deserved one more shot. It turned out to be a shot in the arm.

"Me and my wife and my oldest son, Joshua, got in a little Beretta with about $900 to our names and drove from Houston to British Columbia, Vancouver," Armstrong said. "Everything we owned was inside that little blue Beretta. We went up there with our faith in God, and I believed that He was going to make a way for us. Either that, or my football career was going to be over. Things worked out, and before the season was over, I moved to middle linebacker. One week, I was the CFL Defensive Player of the Week, and my career just began to take off from there."

His career was going exceptionally well in '99 after he was traded to Winnipeg. He became a star for the Blue Bombers in '99, and he was having a career season in 2000 until he broke his leg again on October 15—his birthday. His leg didn't heal correctly, but when the cast came off, Armstrong returned to action and helped lead the Blue Bombers to the Grey Cup (championship) game on a bad leg. He then returned to College Station for another surgery, and up until the summer of 2002 was hoping for one more shot at the NFL.

But the call from the NFL never came, and Armstrong began pouring more time and effort into his nutritional sales company, his personal training and, of course, his growing family. Business is going exceptionally well, and his family is thriving. But Armstrong knows that life is filled with peaks and valleys. And if he is thrown another curve, he's prepared to handle it.

"I've overcome a lot of situations," Armstrong said. "But it has definitely made me a stronger person. I think I'm better equipped now than ever before to handle and conquer anything that comes my way."

His oldest son certainly agrees. Joshua Armstrong is convinced that his father can do anything. And that's probably a fairly accurate assessment.

DERRICK FRAZIER

As a cornerback at Texas A&M and later with the Philadelphia Eagles and Indianapolis Colts, Derrick Frazier always embraced the challenges of man-to-man coverage. Being on an island with an opposing wide receiver often meant there was no one to turn to for help. You either make the play or you make the opponent's highlight reel.

It was a consistent test of his confidence, patience, intellect, toughness, resolve and physical abilities. Playing cornerback, Frazier says, can make you feel like a hero on one play, a goat the next. Such is the nature of single coverage. And, as Frazier has discovered, such is the nature of single parenting. Although he never would have anticipated it when he first started playing the position, cornerback was actually somewhat of a training ground for his role now as a single father. It's sometimes a lonely, thankless job, but it also produces some of the most rewarding moments Frazier could ever imagine.

"I have a little girl whose name is Tia," said Frazier from his home in Houston. "She's 10, and I am raising her by myself. That is a chore in itself, especially because she is a little girl. But she is Daddy's girl, and she is a busy body. She also is more of an athlete than I probably ever expected her to be, to tell you the truth. She loves golf and basketball. I will go out and hit some balls with her, and we have played nine holes before

Photo courtesy of Texas A&M Athletic Media Relations

DERRICK FRAZIER
A&M Letterman: 1989-92

Position: Defensive Back
Second-team All-SWC cornerback in 1992
Third-round draft pick of the Philadelphia Eagles in 1993
Holds school record for passes broken up (36)

together. She is getting to the point where she can make consistent contact with the ball. I know I'm her father, but I think she just might be a future Aggie athlete."

She certainly has the genes to eventually wear the maroon and white. Her father's football career at Texas A&M started slowly, but he finished with an impressive flurry. Frazier still holds the all-time school record for the most career passes broken up with 36 from 1989-92. During his junior season, Frazier teamed with Kevin Smith to form one of the top coverage cornerback tandems in the country. A year later, he joined Aaron Glenn in an equally impressive secondary that also included Patrick Bates.

Frazier, who intercepted eight passes in his A&M career, was a third-round draft pick of the Philadelphia Eagles in 1993, fulfilling a dream that once seemed rather unrealistic. After all, Frazier tipped the scales at a whopping 155 pounds when he first arrived at A&M in 1988. And once he broke into the starting lineup as a redshirt freshman in '89, opposing quarterbacks began picking on him like a bully on the schoolyard blacktop.

But instead of losing his confidence, Frazier continually improved over time. As a senior, offenses still tested him, but Frazier answered the call. After intercepting one pass in each of the first three games of the 1992 season, throwing in Frazier's direction no longer seemed like an attractive option. More than a decade later, Frazier doesn't necessarily recall all the individual moments or plays, but he vividly remembers the magic of playing at Kyle Field.

"Philadelphia is a wild place to play, and I have played in the NFC championship game, Arrowhead Stadium and other so-called great stadiums in the NFL," Frazier said. "I have also played at LSU and other big-time college stadiums. But to me, there is no place like Kyle Field. I've always said that whenever I come back I enjoy it so much because the atmosphere is so different than any place I have ever played. I just remember looking up in the stands and seeing everybody rocking from side to side, yelling their lungs out. You are not going to get that anywhere else in the country. You can go to Michigan where they have 100,000 people and you won't ever see it. You can go to the Super Bowl, and you won't see it. A&M is just a special place in my heart and my memories. To me, it doesn't get any better than A&M, no matter what level you're talking about."

At the next level, Frazier's football career was threatened almost immediately. In the first NFL preseason game he ever played, Frazier picked off a pass on the game's second play. But just as he was proving he belonged, he suffered a serious knee injury, tearing his ACL in the first quarter of his first game. Frazier missed his entire rookie season in 1993, while the Eagles' executives and coaching staff wondered if he was damaged goods. Frazier eased those concerns the following season, rehabilitating his knee and returning to action. Overall, he played five seasons in the NFL—three with the Eagles and two with the Colts.

While playing with the Colts, Frazier was reunited with former A&M teammate Quentin Coryatt. After their playing days came to an end, the native Houstonians formed another team. In 1998, Frazier and Coryatt began discussing the possibilities of producing a magazine together. Originally, they envisioned a publication primarily focused on the Houston market. But the regional concept evolved into a national publication.

Controversy magazine, according to its own website description, is designed "for the man on the go and in the know." It is a mixture of fashion, finance, fitness, entertainment and sports, often taking the controversial slant on its topics. And it is heavily weighted toward the all-time favorite male spectator sport: female watching. While the magazine produced modest profits for Frazier and Coryatt, they sold the publication in 2002. Now, the multitalented Frazier is focused on multimedia.

Frazier recently completed a book called *Find Your Game; Play Like the Pros*. His original vision was to publish the book in typical print form, but he later decided to produce an interactive CD targeted for youths who are seeking an edge for their game. The interactive CD, which was released in the spring of 2004, features plenty of printed tips and pointers. It also includes video clips and interviews from current and former NFL players such as Marshall Faulk, Keenan McCardell and Alfred Williams, as well as former A&M stars like Aaron Glenn, Richmond Webb and Coryatt.

"We developed the interactive CD primarily for kids who can't afford go to $300 a day or $300 a week football camps," Frazier said. "We took everything we have done in camps and all the tips we have experienced in the NFL, college and high school and made a CD for them. We want to try and enhance their game skills and chances of getting college scholarships and giving them the chance to walk-on to a team. We cover everything, ranging from what schools they should look at to walk-on to what position they should try out for and little things that can improve their overall game. I went through a lot of former players, coaches and current players and stockpiled a lot of information that I think will be very valuable to the kids."

Former Texas A&M cornerback Derrick Frazier says being a single father to his daughter Tia may be the most challenging and rewarding endeavor of his life. Frazier, who intercepted eight passes in his A&M career, was a third-round draft pick of the Philadelphia Eagles in 1993. (Photo courtesy of Derrick Frazier)

Frazier says he also has bigger long-term visions for helping kids, including the possibility of beginning a comprehensive sports school in the Houston area to teach the finer points of the games to young athletes. The sports school is still in the infant, planning stages. But the conceptualization of the school, along with the production of the interactive CD, has addressed two of Frazier's primary objectives: helping others and challenging himself.

"Just because I have left the game doesn't mean my competitiveness has decreased any," Frazier said. "God blessed me with some abilities and contacts, and I want to use those things to the best of my ability. I think I have developed a good business sense, and I know I still love to compete and take on challenges."

GREG HILL

A s Greg Hill waits in line to pick up his daughter from her Plano-area preschool, Hill's three-year-old son, Jayden, begins babbling from the backseat. A few moments later, Jordan, his six-year-old daughter, hops in her car seat and delivers a steady flow of chatter regarding her day at school.

Babble and chatter. Gibber and jabber. Banter and chitchat. You get the feeling that Regis and Kelly might be drowned out in this back seat.

"What can I say?" Greg Hill ponders with a chuckle. "They're my kids, and they take after their father. You know I love to talk. Everyone knows I love to talk. I think sometimes I even enjoy hearing myself talk. That's just me; that's just who I am."

Indeed, Greg—or Gregarious—Hill is an outspoken, well-spoken, free-speaking chatterbox, who could probably strike up a conversation with a mime. To the surprise of no one who knows Hill, the former A&M star running back of the early 1990s is making a living primarily because of his unique and animated ability to communicate. Hill's silver tongue has paved the way to an extremely bright future on various fronts.

Prior to the 2003 football season, Hill joined FOX Sports Southwest's college football team as a studio analyst, where he was joined

Photo courtesy of Texas A&M Athletic Media Relations

GREG HILL
A&M Letterman: 1991-93

SWC Offensive Newcomer of the Year in 1991
First-team All-SWC running back in 1991, '92 and '93
Third-leading rusher in A&M school history (3,262 yards)
First-round draft pick of the Kansas City Chiefs in 1994

by his former A&M coach and mentor, R.C. Slocum. The FOX folks were pleased with Hill's development as the season progressed, and he even played a major role in the network winning a Katie Award from the Press Club of Dallas. The award was given to the network for its Lone Star Showdown, a special preview of the annual A&M-Texas game. Toward the end of the broadcast, Hill ripped off his shirt, revealing his old A&M jersey and vowing—in the spirit of the 12th Man—that he would step in for the Aggies if called upon.

"That was great TV," said FOX Sports Southwest general manager Jon Heidtke, also an A&M alumnus. "That wasn't scripted, and he came up with that on his own. Greg had some really good moments for us, and he speaks with a lot of passion. There were also some rookie mistakes he made along the way, but that's to be expected. I know Greg is very serious about continuing to improve, which is not the case with some of the analysts we've had on the air. He has hired a coach to help him improve, and he's committed to getting better. The thing that he can really build on is his passion. He has a ton of passion for the game and a deep passion for Texas A&M."

Hill vows to continue improving his television commentary, but he has apparently already mastered his business communication skills. Even before Hill left the NFL for good in 2000, he became the co-owner of an audio-video business in Dallas. The company did $1.1 million in sales in Hill's first year and $2.3 million the following year before Hill decided to sell his half of the operation. Hill was pleased with his profit, but he was disturbed by what he found in the audio-video industry. Because audio-video equipment is considered a depreciating asset as soon as it is installed in a client's home or office, there were little—or no—financing opportunities.

With his experience in the industry, his business savvy and his gift for gab, Hill began talking to various banks in the Dallas market concerning the possibility of forming his own audio-video financing company. Much like his runs at Kyle Field once did, Hill's presentations immediately netted six—that's the financial backing of six banks. And to borrow another football phrase, Hill then took the ball and ran with it, forming the Hill Capital Group in June 2003. By February 2004, Hill also received the approval of the Custom Electronic Design & Installation Association (CEDIA), the governing body of the audio-video industry in the United States and Canada.

"The financing concept popped into my mind the first time I sat in front of a client, and the client said he had a budget of $30,000," Hill said. "But by the time we sat down and covered all he wanted, it was

$45,000. I can't tell you how many times that happened and how much business we missed out on because of a lack of financing. But I believed in the business plan and made my presentations with a lot of passion. The banks saw the opportunity here, as well, and now every audio-video company in the United States and Canada goes through me to get their contracts financed for their client. And now that I finance audio-video contracts, I thought I needed to sell warranties to these audio-video companies and their clients. I talked to Phillips, the billion-dollar electronics company, and told them what I was doing. They are the ones who sell warranties in the industry, but they weren't reaching their target audience.

"In essence, I am like when you go to the car dealership and buy a $50,000 car. Then they sit you down with the finance manager, who is the one who prepares your financial documents. That is the person who offers you a warranty. Now, that is me for audio-video companies around the country. My company can advise the client what kind of warranty to buy because electronic equipment is going to break, no matter the quality of the product or how good the people are who install it. That sells more warranties for Phillips, and they love it. It's a very exciting opportunity, and it's a real blessing to see how things have fallen into place. I saw an opportunity and seized it."

That was certainly not the first time Hill made the most of an opportunity. Dating back to the first game he ever played in an A&M uniform, Hill has embraced opportunity like a long, lost friend. Hill began his collegiate career in the most impressive fashion of any freshman running back in the history of college football. He earned the starting tailback position when seniors Keith McAfee and Randy Simmons went down with injuries just days prior to the 1991 season opener, and the redshirt freshman from Dallas Carter torched LSU for 212 rushing yards, which is still an NCAA freshman debut record.

With his tremendous speed and outstanding power, Hill parlayed that opening-day performance into a 1,000-yard debut season as the Aggies went 10-2 in 1991 and won the first of three consecutive league titles. Hill was so spectacular as a freshman that fans, teammates and even media members began referring to him simply as "GHT," signifying that it was "Greg Hill Time."

The following year, Hill was even better, rushing for 1,339 yards and becoming the fastest player in SWC history to reach the 2,000-yard rushing plateau. Hill also finished fifth in the nation in scoring in 1992, averaging 8.5 points per game. And the energetic, personable Hill was relishing every minute of his meteoric rise in the A&M record books and the Aggies' national acclaim.

Unfortunately for Hill and the Aggies, 1993 would be filled with almost as much turmoil as triumph. Hill and six other A&M players were cited in an NCAA investigation that involved donor payments for work not performed. Hill quickly and courageously stepped forward to acknowledge his mistake and atone for his involvement. But because of A&M's past track record involving rules violations, the NCAA showed little mercy. Hill was first suspended the week before the 1993 Cotton Bowl and then was forced to sit out of the first four games of the '93 season. When Hill returned to the field in the fifth game of the '93 season, he received a standing ovation from the Kyle Field crowd. It was a mistake that Hill says he wishes he could take back. But he has never dodged the issue and has always accepted responsibility for his actions. And through the years, he has continually proven his love and respect for A&M in his words and his actions.

"When I got in trouble at A&M, that was a very immature mistake I made," said Hill, who in 2000 was one of the first former players to make a financial contribution to A&M's Championship Vision capital campaign for athletics. "I hope everybody knows that I have openly admitted that I was wrong for what I did. Because of the position I was in and who I was, my mistake was magnified. Of course, when you have a school like Texas A&M being punished for the mistakes of individuals, that just magnifies it even more. But the people I talk to on an everyday basis and the Aggies who know me realize it really hurt me deeply to in any way have a negative impact on A&M. Texas A&M helped me to become a man, and it helped make me who I am today. It's where I want my kids to go to school; it's where I devote my time and my money even today. I hope that when Aggies think about Greg Hill, they take everything into consideration and not just one mistake of a 20-year-old kid. I know A&M is a part of me, and I'm even prouder today to be associated with the university than I was when I was in school."

Hill rebounded from the suspension in impressive fashion, rushing for 707 yards in the final seven games and playing a major role in leading the Aggies to their third straight Cotton Bowl. Among his numerous A&M Hall of Fame credentials, Hill is the only running back in A&M history ever to average more than 100 yards per game in three consecutive seasons.

If not for the suspension and his decision to bypass his senior season, Hill almost certainly would have broken Darren Lewis' career rushing record at A&M. But in three seasons, Hill had already proven he was ready for the NFL, where he was a first-round draft pick of Kansas City in 1994. Hill spent four productive seasons with the Chiefs before signing a free agent contract to become the featured back of the Rams prior to the 1998 season.

In St. Louis, Hill began to shine as he did at A&M. He was leading the league in rushing and scoring through the first two games of the season before enduring a broken leg in the third game. It was the first significant injury of his entire football career, and it put his future in jeopardy. Of course, adversity usually brings out the best in Greg Hill, and this time was no different. Hill battled through a painful rehabilitation process and actually gained some speed. The Rams traded him to Detroit, where he started eight games in 1999 and rushed for 542 yards and two touchdowns in his final NFL season.

In perhaps the most memorable game of his final NFL season, Hill starred in the Lions' Thanksgiving Day win over the Bears and was awarded John Madden's famed "Turkey Leg Award," which the TV commentator annually provides to the Thanksgiving MVP. On national television, Hill thanked Madden and dedicated the game to the 12 Aggies who died and the many others who were injured in the Bonfire collapse one week earlier. It was a touching moment that again proved just how much Hill loves Texas A&M.

"When I got hurt, I made it a point to make it back even better than I was before the injury," Hill said. "I have a lot of satisfaction in knowing I did that, and it was such a blessing to be able to stand before America and bring attention to one of the true loves of my life: Texas A&M. God leads my life, and I am so thankful He led me to Texas A&M. Whenever a pitfall or something like that comes along, I know it's God saying I have other plans for you. I've had some tests of my faith, but God is in control. He opened doors for me in football and has continued to open doors for me after my playing days were finished. Now, I have some big dreams for my business and some big goals for my television broadcasting career. It's an exciting time for my family and me."

In other words, it's still Greg Hill Time. And whether he's talking football, talking business, talking about his family or talking up the Aggies, Hill is in his element. Talk may be cheap in some circles, but it's an invaluable commodity to Hill.

Where Have You Gone?

JASON MATHEWS

U pon meeting him, he is so unassuming, so laid back and so utterly unpretentious that it's difficult to imagine Jason Mathews is even involved in the luxury and lavishness of the NFL. That's primarily because—even after 10 NFL seasons—Mathews still finds it hard believe he's playing pro football.

"Never in a million years did I think I would be where I am today," said Mathews, a reserve tackle with the Tennessee Titans and a three-year letterman at Texas A&M from 1991-93. "So I really feel blessed and feel fortunate that I'm even here. I can't really even say this is a dream come true, because to be going into my 11th season in the NFL was way, way beyond even my most far-fetched dreams. I think 99 things had to go right for me to make it, and they all went right. What are the odds of all those things falling into place?"

Probably about the same as Alex Rodriguez receiving a refund from the IRS.

As a freshman from Bridge City High School in 1989, Mathews says he was listed only on the "too-deep" defensive line depth chart. He certainly didn't seem destined for future stardom at Texas A&M back then. And, in fact, he wasn't even originally destined for A&M after he developed into an outstanding high school player.

Photo courtesy of Texas A&M Athletic Media Relations

JASON MATHEWS
A&M Letterman: 1991-93

Position: Offensive Lineman
Originally signed with BYU
First-team All-SWC tackle in 1993
Third-round draft pick of the Indianapolis Colts in 1994

Coming out of Bridge City, Mathews signed with Brigham Young. But it didn't take long to realize that his heart was back in Texas and his heartthrob was at Texas A&M.

"My girlfriend at the time, Kim, who is now my wife, was going to A&M and I felt out of place at BYU," Mathews recalled. "So I called [former A&M head coach] R.C. Slocum. Well, actually my mom called R.C. and asked him if they'd take a look at me. Fortunately, A&M found a place for me. I transferred, and after I sat out that first year, I had hoped to begin my career along the defensive line."

Unfortunately for Mathews, the Aggies then signed some of the top defensive linemen in the country, including Sam Adams and Eric England. So in 1991, Mathews found himself at tight end. While he may have had the body to play tight end, Mathews is the first to admit that he did not have the hands. Prior to 1992, he made another move, to right tackle.

That's where Mathews truly found a home. He earned the starting spot in the third game of the '92 season and never let it go. He helped pave the way for 1,000-yard rusher Greg Hill as the Aggies completed a perfect 12-0 regular season. By his senior season, Mathews was a first-team All-Southwest Conference selection at right tackle. Despite his success, though, the idea of playing at the next level seemed like more of a pipe dream than a plan.

"The NFL stuff was really never even a consideration until the middle of my senior year when they started coming out with all of the mock drafts," said Mathews, who now resides in Nashville. "Some of them had me on there and it was really kind of a shock for me that I was even going to get drafted. But even if I got drafted, I wasn't planning a long NFL career."

Mathews was selected in the third round by the Indianapolis Colts in 1994, and by the 1995 season, he started all 16 regular-season games and three playoff games as the Colts advanced to the AFC title game. By 1997, he'd played in 53 consecutive games, but his career seemed to be nearing an end in 1998 when he first signed with Tampa Bay through free agency but was later waived by the Buccaneers on the final cuts prior to the start of the season.

"Tampa had too many good offensive linemen, and I was really down about getting cut," Mathews said. "I kind of figured it might be over. But every time I think something wrong has happened to me, it turns out to be the best move in the world for me. Tennessee picked me up five days prior to the start of the 1998 season, and a year later we were in the Super Bowl. I love being here. So things obviously happen for a reason. God willing, I'll stay healthy and be able to play at least one more year in 2004. After we got knocked out of the playoffs in 2003, I went to meet with our coaches, and I fully expected them to cut me. But they said they didn't want me to retire and they had me in their plans for 2004. So I'm looking to play at least one more season. Of course, I already feel like I'm playing on borrowed time."

Mathews hasn't been a full-time starter in the NFL since 1996. But he has now played 129 regular-season games. Titans head coach Jeff Fisher has referred to Mathews on several occasions as "one of the best backup tackles in the game." Mathews, who turned 33 in February of 2004, appreciates the praise. But he also realizes the end of his career is drawing near.

"I am still having fun," Mathews said, "but it has been hard for me to go into these last few years thinking, 'Do I keep going when I clearly see that I am not as fast as I used to be?' My body gets so sore and stays sore longer than just a few years ago. On the other hand, I feel like my brain is working better than it used to, because I am seeing things that I didn't see before. I really believe I have a better understanding of the game than ever before, which is why I am thinking that after my career finally ends, I might want to hang around here and get into coaching. It could be with the Titans or at the high school level, but I think that is where I am going to end up."

Mathews and his wife completed construction of their dream home in the Nashville area in 2004, so the couple plans on planting roots in Tennessee for the foreseeable future. The area now feels like home to Jason and Kim Mathews, and it's the only home their children, seven-year-old son Bryce and three-year-old daughter Baylee, have ever known.

But even with his family firmly established in Nashville, Mathews says he longs for the day when he is able to take his children to their first Texas A&M football game. They've grown up around the game and have seen plenty of fanatical fans and goosebump-inducing atmospheres while watching their father play. But Mathews says they haven't seen anything like Texas A&M.

"I was talking to an old Aggie the other day here in Tennessee, and I told him how amazing it was that it has been 11 years since I have seen an Aggie football game in person," said Mathews, who has coached his son's Little League baseball teams in the off seasons. "My son has never seen an Aggie football game, and he would just freak out because there is nothing like it in the NFL. I am probably going to miss playing when I finally retire, but I am already excited about taking my kids to College Station to get the experience of an Aggie game."

Jason Mathews and his wife, Kim, now reside in Nashville with the couple's children, seven-year-old son Bryce and three-year-old daughter Baylee. Entering the 2004 season, Mathews had played 129 regular-season games in his NFL career. (Photo courtesy of Jason Mathews)

Until that day arrives, however, Mathews says he will count his blessings each day for being able to play a decade in the NFL.

"It's really weird because my brother played at McNeese State," Mathews said. "He's four years older than me. This guy did everything right for football. He worked in the weight room and he ate what he was supposed to eat. He was a football machine, and for some reason, he didn't make it in the NFL. Me, on the other hand, I like to play video games. And I'm not the muscular type. I'm not the big, wide body that you expect, and somehow I've made it into the NFL and lasted this long. It's pretty baffling when you see all the great players who didn't make it or didn't stick around for very long. If someone would have told me back in high school that I would eventually start at a great place like Texas A&M and spend 10 years in the NFL, I probably would have laughed in his face."

Instead, Mathews is laughing and smiling at his blessings.

REGGIE BROWN

He's not certain of its exact location, but Reggie Brown knows it's somewhere inside his Austin-area home. He doesn't need it any more, doesn't want it in a prominent location and certainly doesn't plan on playing show-and-tell with it while entertaining guests. Still, like an old box of memories, Brown figures he will probably always hold onto it.

"It" is the halo device that kept his neck and head immobilized for more than a month following a life-threatening, career-altering and perspective-changing injury Brown sustained in 1997 while playing with the Detroit Lions. And until the injury changed his life, Brown had never given a second thought to the appropriateness of the device's name.

Halo. It is most often associated with angels, and Brown believes angels were, indeed, watching over him on December 21, 1997. That's why he's still walking. That's why he is now a father. And that's why he is still alive.

"If I was six inches to the left or right on that play, maybe this would not have happened," said Brown, one of the inspirational leaders of the Aggies in the mid-1990s. "By the same token, if I was six inches to the left or right, I could be dead. It's just part of life as far as I am concerned. Life can throw challenges at you, but it's how you react to them that determines success or failure. In the grand scheme of things, I know I'm very lucky and blessed. I thank God for that."

Photo courtesy of Texas A&M Athletic Media Relations

REGGIE BROWN
A&M Letterman: 1992-95

Position: Linebacker
First-team All-SWC linebacker in 1995
172 career tackles
First-round draft pick of the Detroit Lions in 1996

Brown, who celebrated his 30th birthday in 2004, certainly has plenty of reasons to be thankful. His wife, former Texas A&M women's basketball star Kerrie Patterson-Brown, gave birth to the couple's first child, Reggie II, in 2001. His career also appears to be as rosy as an arboretum. Since 2000, Brown has worked for Pavilion Lincoln-Mercury in Austin in a Ford Motor Company dealer-training program that will eventually enable him to take over a dealership of his own.

Most of all, though, Brown is thankful for life's simple things—being able to walk, to hold his wife's hand, to wrestle with his son and so much more. Ever since Brown lay motionless on the synthetic surface of the Pontiac Silverdome for 17 agonizingly long minutes, he and his wife have seen simple things in a new light.

"I believe everything in our lives is from God," said Patterson-Brown, now the head women's basketball coach at Huston-Tillotson College, a small private school in Austin. "The Lord has blessed us in so many ways, and we are so grateful."

Four days before Christmas in 1997, the Motor City was abuzz with potential playoff excitement as the New York Jets came to town. But that changed in the fourth quarter when Brown, then in his second NFL season, made a tackle, slamming awkwardly into the back of Jets lineman Lamont Burns and pushing his head into Burns's shoulders.

Almost immediately, Brown's teammates realized that he was not moving, and—even more terrifying—he wasn't breathing, either. Paramedics performed mouth-to-mouth resuscitation and later placed a breathing tube down Brown's throat, while players from both teams gathered in mini prayer sessions. And as an ambulance escorted Brown out of the stadium, the steroid methylprednisolone was given to him in massive doses.

The Lions went on to win the game, but in the postgame press conference, neither team seemed interested in discussing the outcome or the playoff implications. The thoughts, discussions and prayers all involved Brown. "If you're a praying person," said then-Lions coach Bobby Ross, "I hope you pray. Hard."

Neurosurgeons later determined that Brown's injury was less severe than initially feared. He suffered a temporary dislocation of the two vertebrae at the top of his spinal column, and when the vertebrae were jarred, they bruised Brown's spinal cord. Any serious spinal injury among the first four vertebrae at the top of the spine can cause breathing loss. Fortunately for Brown, the initial treatment he received on the field and en route to the hospital made a crucial difference.

By the time Brown reached Henry Ford Hospital, he was, according to the director of spine neurosurgery, in "miraculously" good condition. In the hospital, Brown regained consciousness and his surgeons used a pair of two-inch titanium screws to realign his vertebrae, keeping his spine in place. Bone grafts were later added to make sure the fusion was permanent.

When his girlfriend arrived later that evening, the surgery had been a success, and Brown was already being fitted for the halo. Patterson, then a junior at A&M, did not see the injury on television and did not know the extent of the injury until she arrived in Detroit. That was probably a blessing, she says.

Patterson and Brown began dating during Brown's senior year in 1995, when he earned unanimous first-team All-Southwest Conference honors. Patterson was a freshman reserve on the women's basketball team when they met on campus, and it didn't take her long to realize there was something special about the soft-spoken Brown. Even when he was drafted in the first round (17th pick overall) by the Lions in April 1996, Patterson believed it was meant to be.

"I knew I wanted to marry him after two years of dating," she said. "It was hard to continue the relationship when he was in Detroit because of the way people talk about [the wild nature] of athletes. But that's not who Reggie is. And it was easier because he made a strong commitment to us."

Patterson was planning on being in Detroit to spend Christmas with Brown in 1997, and she was already on a flight from Alaska—where the Aggie women were playing in a tournament—when the injury occurred. It wasn't until she left her teammates to catch a flight to Michigan that she first heard about the injury.

"During a layover, I called my parents to let them know how I was doing," she said. "My dad asked me, 'How is Reggie?' I didn't know anything about it. He told me that they took him off the field in an ambulance, and I was thinking he had a stinger because he had been complaining of a stinger. Then when I got on the flight to Detroit I heard some men on the plane talking about it. Still, I wasn't thinking it was something very severe until I got to the airport in Detroit. Reggie had someone pick me up, and when I got into the limousine the guy was driving 120 mph with blinking lights. I thought, 'OK, this is something serious.'"

Neurosurgeons use an index to measure motor function in which 100 is the benchmark for a healthy, mobile person. Brown measured at a zero immediately after the injury. But when Patterson saw her future

On December 21, 1997, Reggie Brown endured a life-threatening neck injury in the Detroit Lions' game against the New York Jets. Brown, who is now married with one child in Austin, has held on to the halo device he was forced to wear following the injury as a reminder to keep things in perspective. (Photo courtesy of Texas A&M Athletic Media Relations)

husband for the first time, he didn't seem to be as worried about his long-term prognosis as much as the couple's immediate plans.

"When I walked in, his first words were, 'I'm sorry,'" Patterson-Brown recalled. "He was sorry because we had planned on driving back to Texas together. I was just thankful that he was alive. But I believed that God was in control. That was definitely a test for our faith, but even then I knew that Reggie is a strong man and felt confident that whatever problem we were going to have to face, I knew we both could handle it.

"He walked two days afterward. He kind of looked like our child when he started walking, but he was still walking. I totally feel that Reggie is blessed and, to me, he is phenomenal because of the things he has faced in his life. Going through that made us have a stronger relationship and gave us a different perspective on life."

Within 48 hours of being paralyzed, unconscious and not breathing, he was taking baby steps. And by early January, he shocked the Detroit media at a press conference when he sprang from a wheelchair, walked to the podium and announced that he would be OK. His football career was over, but his "normal" life was moving forward.

"The thought of never walking again did go through my mind, but it happened so fast because I walked two days after my surgery," Brown recalled. "It wasn't like it was a month or even a week. My total recovery time was six months.

"Even though things were going well, every step of the way was an obstacle. I started out trying to brush my own teeth. I had to start from ground zero. I knew how to do it mentally, but I couldn't physically get it done until my body started coming back to me. I remember my first workout attempt was to bench-press a broomstick about the second week after the injury. It felt like the heaviest thing on earth."

Brown, who bench-pressed nearly 400 pounds before the injury, continued his steady progress throughout 1998. He returned to A&M in the summer of '98 to finish his degree, and, upon earning his diploma, contacted William Ford, the owner of the Lions, about a possible role with the organization. Instead, Ford helped to place him in the dealer-training program that now has him on a fast track to success.

"You work at a dealership for so long and then fly back and forth to Detroit to attend various training seminars," Brown said. "They have a classroom set up where you learn about the different departments of the dealership so that you can eventually run one on your own."

Brown says he isn't opposed to moving out of state, but he hopes that he will land a dealership in Texas. Regardless of where the next move takes him and his family, however, Brown knows that he will probably be packing up the halo and carrying it with him for the next destination.

"I don't know exactly what I want to do with it, but I keep it to have something to reflect upon," Brown said of the halo. "It's one of the reminders I have that keeps things in perspective. I've had my selfish moments when I watch games on TV and think, 'Why me?' I'd obviously love to still be playing. But overall, I feel so very lucky. Things could have ended much differently."

Instead, only his football career ended. The rest of his blossoming life has just begun.

Where Have You Gone?

COREY PULLIG

Still as fit as the day he walked off Kyle Field for the final time, Corey Pullig stepped onto the par-3 tee box and lifted a beautiful 9-iron that landed on the green and rolled some 10 feet beyond the pin. Pullig then casually pulled his tee out of the ground and walked back toward his playing partners in the four-man scramble.

"Nice shot, Corey," said former offensive lineman and A&M teammate Chris Ruhman. "But put a little backspin on the damn thing next time, will you? If you'd put it a little closer, we wouldn't all have to get out of the cart."

Apparently, some things never change. Ruhman, of course, was joking. But there was a rather symbolic appropriateness in his playfully sarcastic comment. Throughout his playing days at Texas A&M, Pullig was often as steady as a marathoner's pace. But even in the long run, Pullig never seemed to do quite enough to appease the masses.

Based on career victories as a starter, Pullig was among the nation's most elite leaders of his time. His 33 career victories from 1992-95 were-matched during that span only by Nebraska's Tommie Frazier, who is still revered in Cornhusker country. Based on career yards, Pullig is the most proficient passer in A&M history, throwing for 6,846 yards in an era

Photo courtesy of Texas A&M Athletic Media Relations

COREY PULLIG
A&M Letterman: 1992-95

Position: Quarterback
Winningest quarterback in A&M history (33-6-1 as a starter)
Leading passer in A&M history
Total offense leader in A&M history
23-1 record as a starter at Kyle Field

when the Aggies sometimes viewed "pass" as a four-letter word. He also ranks as the school's leader in total offense and career completions.

Yet for all he accomplished, Pullig may be the most underrated quarterback in A&M history. In an age of Internet message boards, Pullig is rarely mentioned in the same breath as Kevin Murray, Bucky Richardson or Edd Hargett. That probably has everything to do with timing. Murray, Richardson and Hargett each captivated Aggieland by leading A&M to Southwest Conference titles. But by the time Pullig emerged under center, winning the SWC was no longer enough to quench the thirst of A&M fans. Especially in Pullig's senior season in 1995, the Aggie faithful expected to climb the national title mountain.

Instead, those dreams died in the Rocky Mountains. With a No. 3 national ranking, the Aggies went to No. 7 Colorado on September 23, 1995 and lost one of the most agonizing games in recent school history. A&M never fully recovered from the frustrating loss to the Buffaloes, and Pullig was labeled by some as a quarterback who couldn't win the "big one." In reality, though, Pullig played well enough to win most of the big ones, including that one. It was his supporting cast that literally dropped the ball. One receiver dropped a potential touchdown pass and another A&M wideout let a pass slip through his hands, resulting in Pullig's lone interception of the day and a CU touchdown in the Buffs' 29-21 win.

"It bothered me at the time, but I don't hold grudges," Pullig said of the negative press and harsh labels. "Looking back, I wouldn't have traded my time at A&M for anything. I don't think it ever came out publicly at the time, but I thought about transferring after my sophomore season when [offensive coordinator] Bob Toledo was fired. He and I were really close, and I really respected him as a person. But I'm glad I stayed, and I'm glad I graduated from Texas A&M."

So were his teammates. What often goes overlooked about Pullig was his presence on the field. He wasn't a "rah-rah," boisterous leader in the locker room. Nor was he an animated press conference performer. But he definitely commanded the respect of his teammates.

"Corey Pullig exemplifies what an A&M quarterback should be," said NFL tight end Hunter Goodwin, a former teammate and roommate of Pullig's. "He was a great performer on the field, a great role model off the field. In my opinion, he is probably the most underappreciated athlete in the history of A&M. All he did as a quarterback was win. I could never understand why he wasn't a so-called crowd favorite because he was very diligent and always came prepared. I think maybe our fans were spoiled by how many wins we were getting at that time. He had the utmost respect of his peers. His leadership in the huddle is something that we looked up to and admired. He was the field general."

To those who know him, it comes as no surprise that Pullig, who turned 30 in 2003, is still a leader of men. He was commissioned as a second lieutenant in the Marine Corps in the summer of 2003 and graduated from South Texas Law School in May 2004. Upon passing his Bar Exam, the "good Ag" will become a JAG (Judge Advocate General). Throughout the rigors of officer candidate school, Pullig—as he did so many times in an A&M uniform—continuously proved his mettle.

"I always had an interest in serving my country, but with football I never really had the time," Pullig said. "Going through the process was pretty brutal, but it was tremendously rewarding. I admired the quality of people in the Marine Corps, and I enjoyed the challenges. It wasn't harder than anything I had gone through in football or at home, for that matter. I grew up with three older brothers, and I endured plenty of mental and physical challenges as a kid. But it was a different type of challenge.

"After I pass the bar, I will be back into the Marine Corps full time. I will then be a lawyer in the Marine Corp. One of the things that attracted me to the Marine Corps is that just because you're in the JAG, it doesn't mean that you couldn't still lead troops. That was very appealing to me in case I don't like practicing law in the Marine Corps. There is always that option of going back to do something ground-affiliated."

Pullig has made a practice of keeping his options open ever since he departed A&M. He had several tryouts with NFL teams in '96, but received some misleading information from agents that cost him a serious chance in the NFL and in NFL Europe. So without a job in football, Pullig went to work as a consultant in the technology industry. He then moved into sales and still kept alive his dream of playing pro football. He was participating in a workout for NFL Europe when an Arena Football League coach spotted him and asked him if he would consider the indoor route.

Pullig played well in two seasons with the Grand Rapids Rampage, but he injured his throwing hand both years. During the off seasons, he worked in the marketing and community relations departments for the AFL team and its minor league hockey team, as well. But after two full years in Michigan, Pullig asked Grand Rapids not to protect him in the supplemental draft. The Deer Park native wanted to return to the Houston area, and he decided that if he was going to continue playing in the AFL, he might as well do it for the Houston franchise.

Lisa Pullig convinced her husband to follow through on his law school dreams after the couple met in San Antonio. As he was in his days at Texas A&M, Pullig is still the leader of men. Pullig is now part of the Marines' JAG (Judge Advocate General's Corps). (Photo courtesy of Corey Pullig)

"Instead, Buffalo picked me up, and my boss talked me into taking a leave of absence and going to do it," Pullig said. "I went and played in Buffalo for two months and dislocated my thumb again, and I thought someone was trying to tell me something. At that time my boss was trying to promote me to a management position in San Antonio. I just left Buffalo and came back to San Antonio."

In San Antonio, Pullig met his wife, Lisa, who convinced him to follow through on the law school visions he had been pondering. The couple then moved back to Houston, where Pullig is preparing for full-time duty in the Marine Corps. As for his legacy at Texas A&M, Pullig says he doesn't spend time worrying about it.

"I had really good times at A&M and made some pretty good friends," he said. "But I guess being the type of person that I am, I tend not to dwell on the past. People are going to think what they are going to think. I hope they view me in a positive light, but I can't control that. I'm proud of all the things we accomplished. For the most part, that was a fun chapter in my life."

The next chapter—the Marine Corps and the JAG—is perhaps a perfect fit for Pullig, who has been tested under fire and sharpened by scrutiny. Pullig could easily be bitter, but he's not. He could be arrogant about his accomplishments, but he isn't. He's mature, professional, complimentary and genuinely thankful for his time at A&M.

In 1992, the year Pullig debuted for A&M, one of the most popular movies was *A Few Good Men*. The film could be a preview of Pullig's future role in the JAG, but it's also an accurate description of his past at A&M. Pullig may not be a fan favorite in some circles, but he's earned the respect of those who matter most.

"He's certainly one of the best to have ever played the position at A&M," said Hargett, an All-Southwest Conference quarterback for the Aggies in 1967-68. "He's the winningest quarterback in Aggie history, the leading passer and so forth. His legacy should reflect that he was one of the best of the best."

HUNTER GOODWIN

Hunter Goodwin walks into a crowded social gathering on the Texas A&M campus and immediately begins working the room like he is seeking votes or campaign contributions. Goodwin's strikingly attractive wife, Amber, stays by her husband's side as long as she can before eventually being bumped to the outer circle by Hunter's well-wishers and hand-shakers.

"I'm used to coming to parties or A&M functions as a couple and hooking back up with him as we're about to leave," Amber Goodwin says. "He usually attracts a crowd at something like this, and people love to hear what he has to say."

Like the old E.F. Hutton commercials, when Goodwin speaks, people listen. Especially Aggies.

And Goodwin usually has something to say that is worth repeating, paraphrasing or at least pondering. The man has a stance on so many issues that he could easily be a politician—except for the fact that he has such a complete disdain for political correctness. Goodwin calls everything as he sees it, and there's not a phony bone in his six-foot-five, 270-pound body. He's as easy to read as Dr. Seuss, and you know precisely where Goodwin stands on anything from capital investments to capital punishment by simply leading him down that conversational path.

Photo courtesy of Texas A&M Athletic Media Relations

HUNTER GOODWIN
A&M Letterman: 1994-95

All-Lone Star Conference tight end at Texas A&I in 1992
First-team All-SWC offensive tackle in 1995
Fourth-round draft pick of the Minnesota Vikings in 1996

"What you see is what you get with me," said the articulate Goodwin, who will probably miss his ninth NFL season after injuring his hip in a spring 2004 mini-camp with the Atlanta Falcons. "I've never pretended to be someone or something that I'm not. You take a lot of traits from your parents. Some are not so good and some are really good. My dad always taught me that if you really believe in something or feel strongly about a subject, don't be afraid to talk about it and don't be afraid to voice your opinion. I have tried to take that approach throughout my life. I am not saying I am always right because I am wrong a lot of the time. But if I believe in something passionately, then you are going to hear about it whether you like it or not."

That philosophy has made Goodwin somewhat of an unofficial spokesman about one of his most passionate subjects: Texas A&M athletics. When the Aggies have been good, Goodwin has often served as an obnoxiously enthusiastic supporter of the various programs. But when several major sports took a significant dip at the turn of the 21st century, Goodwin wasn't afraid to publicly voice his disappointment with the overall direction of the athletic department.

Goodwin didn't vent his frustration toward any specific individuals, but his newspaper and radio comments did ignite a landslide of discussions and rants on Internet web sites and in front of water coolers. The theme of Goodwin's message was that Aggies should never settle for mediocrity. Within a calendar year of making his comments, A&M had hired a new athletic director and taken the athletic department in a completely different direction.

Goodwin initially received as much criticism as praise for voicing his opinions publicly. But he points out that he doesn't mind serving as the lightning rod of discussions regarding how to improve Texas A&M. His alma mater means so much to him that he isn't afraid to ruffle feathers, step on toes or to be perceived as the occasional agitator.

"I do believe in A&M passionately because it is the basis for all of my success," Goodwin said. "I am firmly convinced that if I would have gone to a different school, I would not have had the same success I do now. Coming to A&M taught me how to be a man and how to grow up and live responsibly. I've had so many positive influences in my life as a direct result of coming to A&M. By and large, the people I came in contact with at A&M taught me to never settle for second best and reinforced my belief to speak up for causes I believe in. I believe in Texas A&M."

The irony of that statement is that Goodwin once fully believed he was destined to be a Texas Longhorn. Goodwin's father, charismatic

Bellville lawyer/rancher Bob Goodwin, played for UT and raised both his son and older daughter, Amy, as major Longhorn fans. But the Goodwins were first disenchanted by UT's lack of interest in Amy, who was a Class 3A record setter in the 800- and 1,500-meter runs at Bellville High School and later went on to earn All-America honors at USC. Then, when Hunter decided to transfer to a Division I school after two outstanding seasons at Texas A&I (now Texas A&M-Kingsville), he was quite disturbed by the Longhorns' cool reception.

"Attending Texas was a lifelong dream for my sister and me," Goodwin said. "My sister is a better athlete than I am, and Texas did a poor job of recruiting her. They took her for granted since my father was a former athlete and attended UT's law school. They really didn't make her feel wanted, so she jumped ship and went to USC. It wasn't the same for me because no one really wanted me, and I just wanted an opportunity to play. So I knocked on their door first, but I really didn't like the way I was treated in Austin. I have to give Coach [R.C.] Slocum credit because he was really receptive and received me with open arms. He gave me an opportunity when he didn't have to, and I just tried to make the most of it."

Goodwin did just that. After making the switch from tight end to tackle and redshirting in 1993 following his transfer from A&I, Goodwin earned seven starts as a junior in 1994. He then became one of the more vocal leaders of the team as a senior, starting every game at right tackle and earning first-team All-Southwest Conference honors. Goodwin's hard-nosed, aggressive style of play was a perfect fit for the Aggies, and Aggieland was an ideal match for his country boy, conservative personality. And when he wasn't making contact on the field, he was making contacts on campus and in the community. Offensive linemen typically blend into the background, but Goodwin's grit on the field and his appealing personality off of it made him as high-profile on the A&M campus as Reveille.

Even after his A&M playing days were complete, Goodwin left a lasting impression on Texas A&M's former students when, upon signing his first NFL contract, he made a sizeable financial contribution to the 12th Man Foundation, the athletic fundraising organization of Aggie athletics. He has continued to be a leader within that organization's membership, encouraging other former A&M athletes to give back to the program. He has also become somewhat of a role model/mentor to A&M athletes and young NFL players in terms of his financial responsibility. While he is certainly not making front-page headlines with his salary figures, Goodwin has done well financially.

Since entering the NFL following his final season at A&M in 1995, Hunter Goodwin and his wife, Amber, have become involved in real estate investments in the Bryan-College Station area—first with residential developments and now with commercial properties. (Photo courtesy of Hunter Goodwin)

But instead of flaunting it, he's made a practice of investing it. Goodwin says he would like to take full credit for his financial responsibility. But as with his quick wit, passionate opinions and engaging personality, he says he has his parents to thank.

"When players get their first paychecks, they're tempted to run out and spend it on everything they ever wanted," said Goodwin, a fourth-round draft pick of the Minnesota Vikings in 1996. "We all fall into that trap early, but I have been very fortunate to have strong parents that kept me grounded. They really kept a thumb on my back and made me learn to be financially disciplined. My dad actually controlled my finances for the first couple of years I was in the NFL, and he just gave me a little allowance to live off of. Eventually, as I proved my worth, he handed over the reins. Early on, I didn't exactly like it, but in looking back, it was a wise thing because it taught me to have discipline and not to live for instant gratification. It taught me to go out and work for something that you really want. You will enjoy it more if you put in the time and hard work to buy it."

Nowadays, Goodwin is primarily interested in buying real estate. During his first few years in the NFL, Goodwin returned to College Station each off season to work toward finishing his degree, which he received in 1999. But in recent years, Goodwin has become more and more involved in real estate investments in the Bryan-College Station area—first with residential developments and now with commercial properties. Real estate started as a hobby for Goodwin, but now he believes it could become a full-time livelihood when his NFL career comes to an end.

Of course, Goodwin continues to keep all of his future options open. He says he never would have initially envisioned being able to play nine NFL seasons, especially since he averaged less than five catches per year in his first eight seasons in the league. But Goodwin, who spent three years as his team's NFL Players Association team representative, has proven to be a key role player and team leader in both his stints with the Vikings (1996-98 and 2002-2003) and his three seasons with the Miami Dolphins (1999-2001). And even though he may miss the 2004 season because of the hip injury, Goodwin isn't ruling out the possibility of playing again.

"I don't really like to limit myself to how many more years I want to play," said Goodwin, who is also an avid outdoorsman. "I am just try-ing to keep my mind open and stay in shape. I think I could possibly play another couple of years, but I try not to think about it in such a manner. I take it a year at a time and re-evaluate the situation at the end of each year. I like to see how I am physically at the end of each year, along with other factors I consider."

When his playing days do finally come to an end, Goodwin will undoubtedly dive passionately into whatever business venture piques his interest. He says that will also probably be the time when he and his wife begin having the children their family members have been begging and pleading for through the years.

"There is definitely a family ahead of us, but nothing is planned in the immediate future," Goodwin said. "We have gone at our own pace, for which we have taken some heat from both sides of our family. They really don't understand. But we live a unique lifestyle in that we move back and forth from one city to another every six months. I think it would bring undue added pressure to my wife and to me to bring kids into that environment. That's why we have postponed things. We believe it would be better to wait until we have a steadier lifestyle that is more concrete. But we love kids and love the idea of having kids of our own."

And, of course, Amber Goodwin loves the idea of having some family companionship while her husband is moving and shaking in a crowd. It's the crowd that Hunter Goodwin always seems to draw, whether in his stance on a football field or in taking a stance on the topic at hand.

Where Have You Gone?

DAN CAMPBELL

A s a student-athlete at Texas A&M, Dan Campbell was once required to write a research paper on leadership. He could have chosen anyone as his subject—from Gen. George S. Patton or Winston Churchill to Honest Abe and Stormin' Norman Schwarzkopf. Campbell considered a number of possibilities before eventually deciding to write his paper on NFL head coach Bill Parcells.

After all, Parcells was Campbell's kind of guy: A tough, no-nonsense leader who had little patience for losing and absolutely no tolerance for whining, finger-pointing or laziness. Campbell played the game like he possessed a chip on his shoulder and a burr in his jock strap. On the field, he was as intimidating as a biker bar, as volatile as a pit bull and as relentless as a dripping faucet. In other words, Campbell played the game exactly like Parcells coached it.

"He was the first name that popped into my head when we were given the research assignment," said Campbell, the emotional leader of the Aggies' 1998 Big 12 championship team. "I had always been fascinated with him, even when I was in high school. I would see him do interviews and coach on the sidelines and think, 'That's my kind of coach.' He was a winner. I wrote the paper and learned a little more

Photo courtesy of Texas A&M Athletic Media Relations

DAN CAMPBELL
A&M Letterman: 1995-98

Position: Tight End
1998 Aggie Heart Award winner
Captain of the 1998 Big 12 championship team
Third-round draft pick of New York Giants in 1999

about him and his style. I'm not sure how good the paper was, but I enjoyed writing it."

Now, Campbell and Parcells are attempting to write history together. Following three straight 5-11 seasons from 2000-2002, the Cowboys hired Parcells to right the ship in Dallas prior to the 2003 season. One of the Cowboys' first acquisitions under Parcells was the hard-nosed Campbell, through free agency. Dallas then punched almost all the right buttons in 2003, going 10-6 and making the playoffs for the first time since 1999. So the question is: Which was the bigger off-season addition—Parcells or Campbell?

"You'd probably have to give the slight edge to Parcells," Campbell said with a laugh. "But you can call me 'Little Tuna.' I do think I was a part of the turnaround. Obviously, I was one of the players on this team, but before I ever got here there was a good nucleus. Of course, when you bring in the best coach in the NFL, it's going to give a team the spark that needed to happen. I was one of those guys that liked his system and believed in what he believed in. I believed in his discipline and accountability. I grew up that way. If you do something wrong, then you're going to get disciplined for it. If you work hard and do what you are supposed to do, then there won't be any problems. That's the way it is around here now. A lot of guys that were free agents were scared to come here because of Parcells, but it was a perfect fit for me. You know without a doubt that Bill is going to be intimidating, and you are going to have to work your butt off. But that's the way I like it, and I'm thrilled to be in Dallas."

He's also ecstatic to be back in Texas. Campbell grew up as a Cowboys fan, and as a kid, he dreamed of one day wearing the silver and blue. That dream became even bigger after spending his first four NFL seasons with the New York Giants. Despite several injuries early in his pro career, Campbell made a big impression on the Big Apple's sports fans, catching 20 passes and starting all 16 games in 2002. Jeremy Shockey made headlines, but Campbell evolved into one the team's locker room leaders. Campbell says he generally liked the Giants' organization, but he never felt comfortable in New York/New Jersey.

When Campbell was growing up, the nearest "big" city was Glen Rose (population of approximately 2,500). Throughout his four-year stay with the Giants, Campbell felt like a fish out of water or like a dirt road amid a sea of pavement and skyscrapers.

"I remember driving into Manhattan one day at 1:30, knowing that I had to get out of there by 3:00," Campbell recalled. "I needed to do a little shopping, and I spent forever looking for places to park. I finally pulled in this place and they say I can't park there because my

Tahoe is too big. By this time it was 2:30, and I had been driving around for an hour. I finally went to a parking garage, where I had less than an inch of space on either side of my mirrors. Another guy comes running up and says, 'You can't park here.' As calmly as I could, I said, 'I'll pay double, triple, whatever. Just put it in two parking spaces.' I threw him the keys and left. It basically took me an hour and a half just to park my stinkin' truck.

"New York can be a zoo. It sure as hell wasn't like Glen Rose. And to think, I used to get frustrated at traffic in College Station. I was very much out of place in New York, and I'm thrilled to be back in Texas where I belong."

Campbell knew he belonged at Texas A&M almost from the start of the recruiting process, although he now admits there was a time when he gave serious consideration to attending the University of Texas. He had a cousin who had gone to UT, so Campbell was at least intrigued about the possibility of becoming a Longhorn. Campbell was as country as a cotton patch, so, deep down, he knew A&M was probably a better fit. But that realization wasn't cemented in his mind until a Texas assistant coach visited his home and left quite an impression on Campbell's family.

"During recruiting season in 1994, I was getting recruited by all of these schools, and A&M was at the top of the list, and my parents loved A&M," Campbell said. "But I was still thinking about Texas when Bucky Godbolt, the running backs coach at Texas, came to watch basketball practice and said, 'Hey, I'll follow you home, and we'll eat and talk to your parents.' We were about 30 minutes from my high school to where I lived, which is in the middle of nowhere. You drive on a one-lane road for a while and then hit a dirt road. We're driving, and our neighbor's Spanish goats got out. They were always around the creek bed. We are going across the creek, and we cross over and there were the Spanish goats. We finally get to the house, and I get out and mom and dad come out of the house and we are all standing there. Bucky gets out of his truck real slow, and his eyes were as big as silver dollars. He looked at us and said, 'I've never in my life seen black deer like those.' My dad whispered into my ear, 'If he doesn't know the difference between deer and Spanish goats, you're not going to Texas.' And as it turned out, A&M was the perfect place for me."

Campbell was certainly in his element in College Station, helping the Aggies to the 1997 Big 12 South title and leading A&M to the '98 Big 12 championship. He caught 27 passes during his career at A&M, but he was most valuable as the driving leader in the locker room, weight

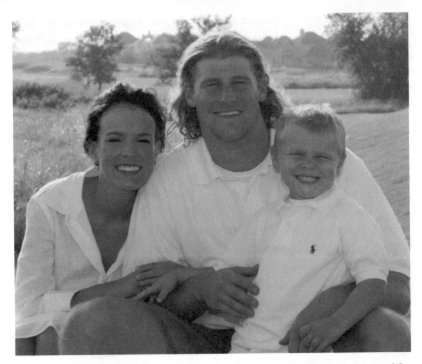

Dan Campbell says he felt completely out of place in New York, but he and his family are back in their element in the Dallas area. Campbell, with wife Holly and son Cody, helped to lead the Cowboys back to the playoffs in 2003, his first season in Dallas. (Photo courtesy of Dan Campbell)

room, practice fields and all other places. Campbell never minced words and was never afraid to speak his mind.

"He was the spokesman for our team and said whatever needed to be said," said 1998 Lombardi Award winner Dat Nguyen, now the starting middle linebacker for the Cowboys. "And look at him now. He's already the spokesman of the Cowboys."

Campbell has definitely become one of the most quotable Cowboys. In fact, in his first season in Dallas, the candid Campbell hosted his own weekly radio show, which drew rave reviews and high ratings in the Dallas-Fort Worth market.

"Originally, I was just going to host the first four weeks of a 16-week show," Campbell said. "When I agreed to do that, this guy from the station asked me to do the entire season. Keep in mind I am not a big-timer by any means. I always thought it was only people like Emmitt Smith, Deion Sanders or Troy Aikman who got their own shows. I felt like I was a little too worthless to be on this show. But I agreed, and within a week or two, the thing took off. I had a good time, and I had other players come on the show with me. Obviously, my first guest was Dat and my last guest was Dat. I have had so many people say, 'Would you have done this up in New York?' I said, 'Shoot no, because my personality and my humor don't match up there in New York.' I would say stuff up there and have people looking at me saying, 'You idiot.' My humor only goes over in Texas."

Campbell says he would love nothing more than to finish his NFL career in Dallas and remain in Texas for the rest of his life. Of course, the five-year NFL veteran is a long way from pondering retirement. Campbell says he believes he is now becoming a much better football player as he becomes a more balanced man. In July 1999, Campbell watched as his wife, Holly, gave birth to the couple's first child, Cody Allen Campbell. Ever since then, Campbell has possessed a different focus on and off the field.

"Being a father does give you a new perspective on life," Campbell said. "It is funny because I think a lot about when I was in high school and in college. I remember being out of control and a ball of emotions. When we lost in high school, I would cry and throw chairs around the locker room. It wasn't healthy. Even in college, I was that way. Things really ate me up. But when Cody was born, it made me realize I had to get control of my emotions. I don't want him picking up those things from me. I didn't lose the fire, but I've learned to contain it and keep it on the field. For so long, my life revolved around nothing but football. But then I get married and I have Cody, and it is just totally different. I feel myself being more focused on football when I'm there, but leaving football at the office, so to speak, when I'm home. Everything just seems so much better, my priorities are right, and I enjoy it and I love it to death right now."

Fatherhood has been so good for Campbell that he and Holly have discussed the possibilities of having another child in the near future. "But every time we talk about it, Cody breaks something else in the house," Campbell said. "That delays the talk for another week or two. So instead, we just bought an English Mastiff puppy. When he's completely grown he is supposed to be 200 pounds. That will serve as our second child for the time being."

SIRR
PARKER

L ooking back, Texas A&M fans probably should have recognized Sirr Parker's flair for dramatics from the start. And as far back as National Signing Day in 1995, Aggies should have realized it was never wise to discount the street-tough, wise-beyond-his-years speedster.

On that February morning, as former Texas A&M head coach R.C. Slocum addressed his new signing class with the media, the phone rang. It was Parker, calling to inform Slocum of his last-minute intentions. Slocum, who was on the verge of giving up on the playmaker from South Central Los Angeles, was as giddy as a schoolgirl as he announced that Parker was destined for Aggieland. At that moment, most A&M fans also figured he was destined for stardom.

The recruiting services pegged Parker and Ricky Williams as the top two running backs in California and among the top five in the country. By early February of 1995, both were headed for the Lone Star State and future football fame.

Or so it seemed. While Williams won the 1998 Heisman Trophy and set 21 NCAA records at Texas, Parker struggled through a series of bad breaks and bad luck at A&M. He occasionally displayed flashes of greatness, but he rarely sparkled in the manner he once envisioned.

Photo courtesy of *12th Man Magazine*

SIRR PARKER
A&M Letterman: 1995-98

Position: Running Back
Scored winning touchdown in 1998 Big 12 title game
A&M's leading rusher in 1996
Recorded two 100-yard rushing performances in 1997

Parker shared time in the A&M backfield from 1995-97, and he missed much of the 1998 season with an injured hamstring.

By November 27, 1998—the day Williams dashed and darted through the Aggies for 259 yards to become the NCAA's all-time leading rusher—the San Diego native had become perhaps the biggest legend in Longhorn history. The Los Angeles native in maroon and white, however, had become something of an afterthought.

That changed one week later when Parker forever etched his legacy in Aggie history by producing several monumental plays in A&M's stunning upset of No. 1-ranked Kansas State in the Big 12 championship game. Rallying from a 15-point, fourth-quarter deficit, the Aggies first tied the game with 1:05 left in regulation when Branndon Stewart hit Parker on a nine-yard scoring pass and then found Parker again for the critical two-point play. Then in the second overtime—as no Aggie who witnessed it will ever forget—Stewart hit Parker on a quick slant that turned into a 32-yard touchdown that shocked the college football world.

The stunned Wildcats fans are probably still stinging from that 36-33 loss. And the once-forgotten Parker is still beaming.

"Everything happens for a reason," Parker said from his home in Inglewood, California. "My career at A&M obviously wasn't everything I had hoped for in terms of what I accomplished. When it doesn't work out to the magnitude that you want it to, you wish you could do things over again. But to finish my career at A&M the way I did was very rewarding. During most of my senior season, I nursed a hamstring injury and didn't play as much as I wanted to. But [the K-State game] was just one of those situations that, when you get an opportunity, you have to take advantage of it and make the best of it. That's what Branndon and I both did in that game. It was such a great memory for the school and all the Aggie fans. It was one of those magical days where dreams come true, and I can still see it all unfolding just like it was yesterday."

Since Parker was last seen diving toward the pylon of the TWA Dome in St. Louis, he has bounced around in pursuit of fulfilling more gridiron dreams. As an undrafted rookie free agent in 1999, Parker first landed in San Diego on the Chargers' practice squad. The next year, he was waived and picked up by the Carolina Panthers. Still unable to join the active roster due, in part, to hip and hamstring injuries, Parker was placed on the inactive list and signed to the practice squad again.

Then in 2000, Parker was waived by the Panthers and acquired by the Cincinnati Bengals, who attempted to convert the offensive-minded Parker into a defensive back—a position he had not played since his high school days at Locke. Despite some struggles in the adjustment, Parker started in the secondary during the final three games of the 2000 season.

"It was a real tough move, because I hadn't even backpeddled in I don't know how long," Parker said. "It was a little overwhelming going from offense to defense in the NFL. But it was a dream come true to make it to the NFL. Playing in the NFL was my ultimate goal since the time I started playing when I was eight years old. Hopefully, I can return one day and make it back to the NFL. That's my goal, but even if that doesn't happen, making it there is a lot more than most people can say."

Parker, who also made a run at a roster spot with the Canadian Football League's Calgary Stampeders in 2002, is now playing in the Arena Football League. In 2003, Parker shared a spot in the Dallas Desperados' backfield and a room with former A&M teammate Ja'Mar Toombs. He then was traded from Dallas to the Austin Wranglers prior to the start of the 2004 season. Parker, who will turn 27 on Halloween in 2004, realizes the odds are stacked against his dreams of returning to the NFL. Of course, facing long odds and major obstacles are nothing new to Parker. And no matter what atrocity life has thrown at him, Parker has consistently proven he has the strength to rise above it.

Raised without a father in South Central Los Angeles, Parker grew up to the sounds of gunfire, sirens and drug deals gone bad. And because of his mother's addictions, Parker not only looked out for himself, but also practically raised his younger brother. Despite all his disadvantages and time constraints, Parker managed to be a star running back at Locke, while working a part-time job and maintaining a 3.9 grade point average.

"I use Sirr as an example around school all the time," said Parker's former dean and football coach at Locke, E.C. Robinson. "Kids here make excuses about how their mother is on drugs or their father left home or whatever else. Then I tell them about Sirr. Here's a kid that had worse problems than most of them ever imagined."

Parker's perseverance and positive outlook has been an inspiration at Locke for almost a decade. And in 2001, his moving story went nationwide when Showtime released the made-for-cable movie, *They Call Me Sirr*. Parker says he still hasn't seen the movie, but he has experienced its impact on others.

"I lived it, and [watching the movie] was something I chose not to do," he said. "When I was in high school, the Los Angeles *Times* wrote a cover story on me, and when I first got to college, a guy approached me and said he had read the story and wanted to write a movie about it. It was an ongoing process since I was in college, and it was one of the

State of Texas governor Rick Perry (right), a former Yell Leader at Texas A&M, catches up with another Aggie, Sirr Parker, prior to one of the Austin Wranglers' 2004 games in the Arena Football League. Parker was traded from the Dallas Desperados to the Wranglers prior to the '04 season. (Photo courtesy of the Austin Wranglers)

things that I thought would probably never happen. When it finally did come out, I considered it a great honor. A lot of people ask me about the movie. A lot of adults and elders talk about how it was not just a great inspiration for their kids, but also for them. That means a lot to me, because I would love to help people in any way I can. It is amazing how many people—even people I don't even know—come up to me and talk about how proud they are of me. It is funny to meet people that swear that we did things together. I just keep on smiling. It is actually a privilege to meet some of the people I have met because of the things I have overcome."

When he is not playing in the Arena Football League, Parker returns to Locke High School to help kids coming from similarly difficult backgrounds to overcome their own obstacles. He works as a coach at Locke and says he may be interested in pursing the profession on a full-time basis when his playing career comes to an end.

Parker, who is also pursuing plans of eventually returning to Texas A&M to finish the final 18 hours on his undergraduate degree, is quite a role model to the kids at Locke, as well as his own seven-year-old daughter, Alashea. While his immediate future isn't clearly defined, Parker feels confident that he is on the verge of another career breakthrough. Whether it comes as a coach, a player or in some other capacity, most Aggies share the same belief.

Ever since that February day in 1995, Aggies have learned to admire Parker's ability to overcome obstacles. And they've come to expect Hollywood-like heroics from the L.A. kid whose will to thrive is greater than any obstacle he's ever encountered.

RANDY McCOWN

During his playing days at Texas A&M, former quarterback Randy McCown commanded the utmost respect of 300-pound linemen and future NFL stars, ruling the offensive huddle with a fiery presence that had his teammates hanging on his every word. Those were the days, McCown now says with a laugh.

As the general manager of Cross Cut Hardwood, a lumber company in Alto, he's still the hard-charging, determined leader of men. But at home, the young man who once barked at giants often finds himself begging his two-year-old daughter, Kylie.

"Now that [Kylie] is in my life, I am no longer on my schedule," McCown said. "She definitely rules the roost. It's funny how someone so little can be so demanding."

And that's just the half of it. McCown and his wife, Shellie, welcomed the couple's second child, Patrick Ryan, in April 2004. To the surprise of no one, McCown is totally devoted to fatherhood—just as he was once completely committed to leading the Aggies.

"I think being a father is awesome," McCown said. "You never realize how much it will change and enhance your life until they are here. It seems like your whole attitude changes from working for yourself to working for that little girl or boy, trying to give them every opportunity

Photo courtesy of Texas A&M Athletic Media Relations

RANDY McCOWN
A&M Letterman: 1996-99

Position: Quarterback
Sixth leading passer in school history (4,187 yards)
Longest pass in school history (96 yards in 1999)
Holds school record for most passing yards (2,374)
ever among senior quarterbacks

in the world. It's the most rewarding thing I have ever experienced. It also may be the most challenging, but I've always loved a challenge."

McCown has probably never backed down from a challenge in his life. He certainly never did when he was at A&M, battling first for his job and then overcoming numerous obstacles thrown in his path.

McCown, who lettered from 1996-99, will probably not go down in A&M annals as one of the most talented quarterbacks in school history. But he should be near the top of any list that is categorized by intangibles such as toughness, intensity, determination, heart and hustle.

McCown played the position with as much passion as a stack of romance novels. While some quarterbacks are labeled as dual threats or pure passers, McCown may have best been described as "true grit." He was a good passer, finishing his career as the sixth leading quarterback in school history with 4,187 passing yards. And his 2,374 passing yards in 1999 still ranks as the fourth best single-season total in school history. With a more quarterback-friendly offensive system, those numbers undoubtedly would have been even better.

Regardless, McCown will be most fondly remembered by A&M fans for his relentless, fearless and selfless style of play. He hated the hook slide and preferred to go head first for every extra yard, playing with as much tenacity as touch. In many ways, he personified the 1998 Big 12 championship team, as he was often overlooked, frequently forgotten and regularly underappreciated. But like the '98 Aggies, all McCown did was win. Although he missed the Big 12 championship game after suffering a separated shoulder the week before against Texas, his never-say-quit attitude was vital for the title.

Even though the 1999 season did not turn out as McCown or the Aggies had hoped, it ended in a most memorable fashion. In one of the most meaningful and emotional victories in school history, it was McCown who tossed the game-winning touchdown to his best friend, Matt Bumgardner, to beat Texas eight days after the tragic collapse of the bonfire.

"Most of [the wins] kind of felt the same, but when you step back and look at your last pass at Kyle Field being a touchdown to beat Texas you can't ask for anything better," McCown said. "Especially considering the circumstances of that game and throwing the pass to Bum, I think winning the national title is about the only thing that could top that."

Those memories and the friendships he made at Texas A&M mean more to McCown than even a national title or pro contract could bring. His younger brother, Josh, is now a quarterback with the Arizona Cardinals after beginning his collegiate career at SMU and then transferring to Sam Houston State. And his youngest brother, Luke, is now the starting quarterback at Louisiana Tech, earning the attention of pro scouts in the Bulldogs' pass-first offensive philosophy.

Randy McCown has occasionally wondered how his life might be different today if he had pursued thoughts of transferring to a smaller school after Branndon Stewart was awarded an extra year of eligibility. His passing skills would have certainly been honed in a more open attack, and his pro prospects would have dramatically improved. But in the big picture, McCown has no regrets.

"Honestly, I do think if A&M had thrown the ball more I would have had a better chance [at the pros]," McCown said. "I once thought about transferring. But say if I went to a place like Stephen F. Austin or Sam Houston, I might have gotten a shot, but then I wouldn't have the A&M connections that I have now. I am not just blowing the old maroon and white horn, but I don't think transferring would have outweighed the friends and relationships that I made at A&M. I would do it all over again the same way. I met a lot of great people. When it is all said and done, all the money you could make while playing in the NFL is not as important to me as the friendships and connections I made at A&M that will last forever. You can't put a dollar amount on any of that."

While McCown went undrafted, he did give professional football a try. He jokes that he became a filthy rich millionaire by playing in the Spring Football League, a semi-pro organization that started in 2000 and folded two games into the inaugural season. After that, McCown packed up his money bags and gave the Arena Football League a shot, signing with the Houston franchise in 2000. Initially, things were going exceptionally well, and it appeared as if McCown could emerge as the ThunderBears' starter.

But then Houston signed Todd Hammel, the all-time leading passer in the history of the Arena Football League. McCown then decided it was time to find a real job.

"They signed Hammel, who was like the Dan Marino of the Arena League," McCown said. "He had been in the league forever, and I didn't feel like I was given a fair shot at it, especially since Todd and the head coach had worked together before. After that, I did all the soul searching and praying and just decided it was enough. I went through the preseason, and Bumgardner actually played with me through the preseason, but he wound up being released because of injuries. I don't know if Bum leaving was a sign or what, but I just felt like it was time to go."

Randy McCown and his wife, Shellie, were blessed with their second child, Patrick Ryan (not pictured), in 2004, providing a sibling for Kylie. McCown is now the general manager of Cross Cut Hardwood, a lumber company in Alto. (Photo courtesy of Randy McCown)

McCown grew up around the lumber industry, and once he began searching for full-time employment, returning to it eventually seemed like a natural fit. He is now on a five-year plan to assume ownership of the operation.

"The only reason I got involved with this initially was to have something to do while I was waiting on chances to play football again," he said. "You never understand why the good Lord opens doors, but He just does and they seem to work out. He opened up this opportunity here in Alto and it seemed like a good thing, so here I am.

"I enjoy it some days. It's hard work with what I am doing. There are some days where two-a-days wouldn't be so bad. You are outside, and it's not something where I am just sitting behind a desk all the time. I am definitely out there getting dirty. This is one of those things that you can make good money if you are the owner and that is what I am working toward. So I try to attack this like I am attacking defenders on the football field."

Perhaps that attitude will lead McCown to as much respect in the industry as he once commanded on the football field. Then and now, McCown is a natural-born leader, even though his daughter may still need some convincing.

MARK
FARRIS

Kicked back in a leather lounge chair inside Kyle Field's Zone Club, Mark Farris sipped a cold beer while keeping one eye on Texas A&M's game and one on the television monitors broadcasting other games of interest. It was the midway point of the 2003 season for the Aggies and Farris's first trip back to an A&M game since he last suited up in the maroon and white.

All things considered, Farris found himself completely at ease and quite content in these far more cozy Kyle Field elements.

"This is how to enjoy a football game," Farris said with a satisfied grin. "I could get used to this. I wondered if I was going to miss being on the field, but I don't miss it at all. Not after what I went through the last couple years of my career."

What Farris endured toward the end of his collegiate career was a combination of alienation, exasperation and complete frustration. Almost overnight, Farris descended from rising superstar and fan favorite to forgotten benchwarmer and statistical anomaly. How could the strong-armed, well-respected Farris go from breaking A&M's single-season passing record as a sophomore to serving as little more than a sideline spectator as a senior?

Photo courtesy of *12th Man Magazine*

MARK FARRIS
A&M Letterman: 1999-2002

Position: Quarterback
Fourth leading career passer in A&M history (4,949 yards)
Holds school's single-season passing record (2,551 yards)
First-round draft pick of the Pittsburgh Pirates in 1994

"It's a long, sordid story," says Farris, who now owns and operates a thriving insurance agency in Baytown. "I could practically write a book on all the specific details, but in my opinion, it really all boils down to two words: Dino Babers. The sad thing is that he didn't just ruin my career; when he was hired, it was also the beginning of the end of R.C. Slocum's career. This is just my own opinion, of course, but I really and truly believe that if R.C. Slocum would have hired Kevin Sumlin or practically anyone else as offensive coordinator in 2001, R.C. would still be the head coach at Texas A&M. We certainly wouldn't have gone 6-6 in 2002 if Sumlin was calling the shots the entire season. I'd stake my reputation on that."

Farris's football reputation initially began to skyrocket in 2000, his first year as the Aggies' starting quarterback. After completing nearly 60 percent of his passes for a school-record 2,551 yards as a sophomore, most Aggie fans—and fans throughout the Big 12, for that matter—believed Farris could possibly become the next Chris Weinke of college football. Until the 2002 season, their careers were freakishly similar.

Farris originally signed with A&M in February 1994, joining a recruiting class that included future standouts like Dat Nguyen, Dan Campbell, Warrick Holdman and Steve McKinney. But Farris, also a first-round pick of the Pittsburgh Pirates in the June '94 amateur draft, was enticed into pro baseball by an $830,000 signing bonus. It was an offer he simply couldn't refuse.

But as Farris would soon discover, the life of a low minor leaguer was often more dreary than dreamy. It was made more difficult by a temporary switch in positions (from shortstop to third), a torn ACL in April 1995 and the birth of his first daughter in May '95. Farris recovered from the injury and began a slow climb through Pittsburgh's system, hitting .273 in AA in 1998, his best year in the minors. The grind of long bus trips, cheap motels and constant travel, however, took its toll on Farris and his family. Toward the end of the '98 baseball season, his wife, Neocia, suspected her husband was having thoughts about his first love: football.

"Being a minor leaguer was hard on Mark and the family," Neocia said. "He was chasing a dream, but I could tell it was becoming less of a dream. He would look at guys who were really good that were 30 years old and still in AA ball. They had to stay there because they didn't have other options. Mark always knew he had another option."

On August 31, 1998, inside another forgettable hotel room, Farris flipped on the television and watched something that sealed his decision. Florida State, led by the then-26-year-old Weinke, was playing Texas

A&M in the Kickoff Classic. The Aggies lost the game, but gained their future quarterback.

"I remember watching that game, and by that time I had already started thinking about my future plans," Farris said. "It was near the end of the baseball season, and after I took a little time off, I got in touch with Coach Slocum and told him I was thinking about giving football another shot. He welcomed me back."

Farris's family also welcomed the thought of settling along Highway 6 instead of Motel 6, and in 1999, Farris returned to school, serving primarily as Randy McCown's backup. The following season, the 25-year-old Farris was winging and flinging his way into A&M's record books under the tutelage of offensive coordinator Steve Kragthorpe. At one point in 2000, the Aggies were 7-2 and in the hunt for the Big 12 title. Defensive lapses down the stretch produced a three-game losing skid to end the season, but even with the disappointing finish, the Aggies looked as if they possessed a legitimate building block for the future in Farris.

Prior to the 2001 season, however, Kragthorpe (now the head coach at the University of Tulsa) left for an NFL assistant's job, and Slocum hired Babers as his offensive coordinator/quarterbacks coach. Almost immediately, Farris and Babers clashed like the Hatfields and McCoys. The strain between the coordinator and quarterback played a major role in A&M's offensive nose dive. The '01 Aggies scored just 17 points in their final three regular-season games, and what began as a promising season (A&M was once 7-1) turned into another disappointing finish. An A&M offense that scored 307 points in 2000 and averaged 381.6 yards per game scored just 220 points and ranked 106th nationally in total offense.

On paper, Farris didn't have a particularly bad 2001 season. He passed for 2,094 yards, the sixth best single-season total in A&M history. But especially toward the season's end, he did not resemble the record-breaking quarterback of a year earlier. He didn't seem as comfortable, and while he never mentioned it at the time, Farris now acknowledges he was continually baffled and beleaguered by Babers's play-calling and mind games.

"It was terribly frustrating because we were a much more talented offense than that," Farris said. "Part of playing quarterback is taking the blame. I don't have any problem taking my fair share of the blame, because I didn't play as well as a junior as I did as a sophomore. But so many times our offensive coordinator was not putting us in a position to be successful. I can't tell you how many times in meetings that the offen-

Mark Farris is now operating a thriving insurance agency in Baytown. He and his wife, Neocia, have two daughters, Kendyll and Kameryn. (Photo courtesy of Mark Farris)

sive players had to correct what the coordinator was saying. I recall the Oklahoma game in '01, where we had 61 yards of total offense and two first downs in the final three quarters. Oklahoma's defense was good, but not that good. Put in the tape and watch it. We ran the fullback belly about eight out of 10 plays. Two or three of our offensive linemen, after the third or fourth belly play call in a row, looked at me in the huddle and said, 'Are you freaking kidding me?' That's one example of how bad it was."

There were others. Following the Aggies' first loss of 2001 at Colorado, Babers chastised his quarterback at a press conference for fumbling late in the game when he was blindsided by Colorado's Kory Mossoni. Babers said there were two kinds of quarterbacks: Those who fumbled when they took that kind of hit and those who didn't. Babers said he preferred those who didn't. And three weeks later—after the Farris-led Aggies improved to 7-1—A&M trailed Texas Tech 3-0 at the half. When Babers entered the locker room, he didn't address Farris. Instead, Babers told backup quarterbacks Dustin Long and Vance Smith—in front of Farris—to get ready to go into the game. At the time, Farris was completing 61 percent of his passes, while the other two quarterbacks had not completed a pass during the season.

"I am sitting right there, and I am supposed to go out there and play knowing my coordinator doesn't want me in the game," Farris recalled. "Playing quarterback is such a mental deal, and it's completely different from any position. I'm pretty thick-skinned, but things like that really started to bother me. By the end of that year, I admit that I was mentally wrecked."

Farris was so frustrated that he gave serious consideration to leaving school early and entering the NFL draft. He didn't figure he would be a high draft pick, but his quick delivery and field savvy did have various NFL scouts extremely impressed. But after a little time away and the birth of his second daughter, Farris decided to stay for one more year. It was a decision that would prove to be fatal for his pro football aspirations.

Farris enjoyed an outstanding spring in 2002, and he left two-a-days entrenched as the starter. Even after the season opener in 2002, when the Aggies used three other quarterbacks in relief of Farris in an easy win over Louisiana-Lafayette, Slocum was quoted afterward as saying, "We're looking at a situation a year from now where Mark will be gone and one of these young guys is going to have to be the starter."

One week later, however, Farris would earn the final start of his A&M career. Farris opened at Pittsburgh, but with the offense struggling, he was benched late in the second quarter in favor of sophomore Dustin Long. Farris never played again. Not in the game or the season. It wasn't until Slocum removed the play-calling duties from Babers prior to the fourth game of the season that the A&M offense began to show some life. By that time, Slocum had made the decision to go with a youth movement under center, utilizing Long and the much-heralded true freshman Reggie McNeal.

Long compiled record-setting numbers of his own with Sumlin calling the plays, and McNeal led A&M to a stunning win over No. 1-ranked Oklahoma at Kyle Field. But they also made a ton of rookie mistakes, combining for 19 interceptions in the final 10 games, including several game-breaking picks. The 19 interceptions were more than Farris had in 31 career games.

"The sad thing is that they threw those two guys into the fire too early," Farris said. "Reggie has some unbelievable raw talent, but he wasn't ready as a true freshman. He should have been redshirted. That was really unfair to his development. And Dustin could have learned a lot more by being slowly groomed to be the starting quarterback. But for whatever reason, they really wanted to get Reggie on the field, and I was the odd man out. I'm not saying I would have led us to the Big 12 title in '02, but I wouldn't have made the mistakes late in games that those guys did. I'm not blaming those guys for anything, because I made the same mistakes my first year as a starter. But I truly believe that if I had been the starter in 2002, and if Sumlin had been calling plays all along, we would have been in a nice bowl game."

Instead, the Aggies went 6-6 and Slocum, along with the rest of his staff, was fired at the end of the season. And instead of making an assault on the all-time A&M passing records or signing a professional contract, Farris kept an extremely low profile throughout the 2002 season, never speaking to the media or complaining publicly about being relegated to the bench. Then in December, he graduated with the A&M degree he first envisioned when he signed with the Aggies in 1994. Farris, who turned 29 in February 2004, immediately put the Aggie network to use, hooking up with former A&M walk-on Warren Barhorst (also featured in this book) in the insurance business. Barhorst says that establishing Farris in his own Nationwide agency has been one of the best business decisions he's ever made.

"He's a go-getter and an extremely effective salesman," Barhorst said of Farris. "The guy is so down to earth and unpretentious, but he also has an incredible drive to succeed. He didn't just hit the ground running here; he hit it in full sprint. He has an incredibly bright future in this career."

Farris also appears to be incredibly happy in his new field. His business in Baytown is growing as quickly as his family, which includes nine-year-old daughter Kameryn and two-year-old daughter Kendall. And even when pressed, Farris says he harbors absolutely no hard feelings toward Texas A&M and has no regrets about first returning to A&M in 1999 and then choosing to finish his senior year.

"I don't regret it at all because I love what I am doing right now, and I love working for an Aggie who has been great to me and my family," Farris said. "There are times when I think about how miserable I was and how frustrated I was and wish I could have played a couple more years under Steve Kragthorpe's offense or even been around to be a part of Coach [Dennis] Franchione's first season. But all that's water under the bridge. I am so proud to be an Aggie and so proud to wear this Aggie ring that it makes everything worthwhile. Just walking up to Kyle Field for the first time as a regular guy was very special because of how the fans treated my wife and me. I will always speak very highly of Texas A&M, and I am a big fan of Coach Fran as he turns this thing around. Selfishly, I wish things would have worked out differently for me on the field. But everybody has to face difficult situations and deal with difficult circumstances in life. I'm proud of the way I handled the situation when it was going on, and I'm proud to be an Aggie now. I can already tell I'm going to love coming back for games. These leather chairs are a lot more comfortable than that bench down there. I just hope A&M fans remember me for things other than being benched."

In all likelihood, they'll remember him primarily for setting the single-season benchmark for future Aggie quarterbacks. While Farris did not go out in a blaze of glory, the majority of A&M fans now realize he had more "game" than the game plan often allowed.

Where Have You Gone?

Additional Aggie Greats:
Baseball, Basketball, Track, and Volleyball

AL
OGLETREE

Raised as a baseball fanatic in a Catholic home, a young Al Ogletree once possessed a diamond-clear vision of his future. He wanted to play collegiate baseball, and he wanted—more than just about anything else—to do it at Notre Dame.

Ogletree nurtured that dream throughout his youth, and he let his Austin High School baseball coach, Tony Burger, know about his ultimate goal. Burger, the namesake for Austin's Burger Center, listened attentively and eventually offered Ogletree some "I've been there before" advice.

"He was a second father to me, and he was a heck of a coach," Ogletree said of Burger. "He had gone to Notre Dame, and he told me that if I wanted to play baseball I needed to go someplace where the weather was good. At that time, Marty Karow, who was the coach at A&M, had written me a letter. He was the only one who had really contacted me. That's what led me to A&M, even though I had never even seen A&M. It all worked out for the best."

It actually couldn't have worked out much better. For Ogletree and for Texas A&M.

In Ogletree, the Aggies landed a hard-nosed, hard-charging catcher who would eventually help lead A&M to its first appearance in the

Seventy-four-year-old Al Ogletree resides in McAllen with his wife of 50 years, Joann. The couple has five kids, 11 grandchildren and a great-grandson. (Photo courtesy of Al Ogletree)

AL OGLETREE
A&M Letterman: 1950-52

Sport: Baseball
Position: Catcher
First-team All-SWC catcher in 1951
Texas A&M Athletic Hall of Fame
Drafted in 1952 by the Lake Charles Skippers (Evangeline League)

College World Series. And for Ogletree, Texas A&M served as the training ground for a legendary career in collegiate baseball.

During a decorated coaching tenure, Ogletree won more than
1,200 games and led tiny Pan American College to the College World
Series in 1971. Ogletree, who coached at Pan American from 1969-97,
led the Broncs to at least 40 wins 12 times. He reached the 50-win
plateau seven times and won more than 60 games three times.

"Al is a great baseball man with great passion for the game," said
A&M head coach Mark Johnson, who first met Ogletree in 1976 when
Johnson was an assistant at Arizona. "He knows the game, loves it and is
a great historian of the game. He's been inducted into about every Hall
of Fame that is available to him, and I consider him to be one of the legends in college baseball in this state. He coached [29 seasons] at Pan
American, but I have always known he is an Aggie through and through.
He's always been very proud of his Aggie ring. He's just one of the special, special guys in the baseball fraternity. He's done some great things
in baseball."

One of the greatest memories Ogletree recalls was his time as a student and player at A&M. Following Burger's advice and Karow's request,
Ogletree committed to play for the Aggies and promised to arrive on
campus in the fall of 1948. But before his career in Aggieland began, the
Texas Longhorns made the first of several runs at him. After his graduation from Austin High School, he played in a semi-pro league in Sweeny.
Ogletree was so impressive in the Houston Post Tournament that Texas
coach Bibb Falk made a late sales pitch.

"The night before, I had won the game with a base hit in the bottom of the ninth," Ogletree said. "The next day, Bibb Falk asked me
where I was going to school, and he told me that he wanted me to come
to Texas. He said he would give me tuition, books and would try to get
me a job at C&S Sporting Goods. I don't know if that was legal at the
time, but I told him I was going to A&M. He said, 'OK,' and then he
walked off."

Falk walked away, but Texas didn't give up. In 1949, as Ogletree
was starring on the Aggies' freshman team, UT again made another
attempt to lure him back to Austin. This time, the attempt came from
the top-ranking official in the state.

"When I was a freshman, I hit a grand slam to win a game, and
Gov. Buford Jester was there," Ogletree said. "Gov. Jester had followed
us in high school, and he was one of my biggest fans, and I was one of
his biggest fans. He wrote me a letter after the game and said he wanted
me to come have supper with him in the mansion one day. My dad drove

me to the mansion and stayed in the car while I had steak and strawberry shortcake. It was some kind of meal. After supper, Gov. Jester and I went into his study and he asked me if I had thought about transferring to Texas. I said, 'No, sir. I am committed to A&M.' He said that was all he wanted to know and told me that he had a bunch of calls wanting to know if I was interested in transferring to Texas. When I told my dad about that, I think he was relieved. Apparently, people had been giving him grief about that. I know he wanted me to honor my commitment to A&M."

Ogletree kept his word and soon led the Aggies to a place no A&M team had been before. The 1951 Aggies opened the year by splitting a pair with the Brooke Field Medics and were just 6-4 heading into conference play. And league play certainly didn't begin with many dramatics, as the Aggies were just 3-4 on April 27.

But on the following day against a TCU team that had already beaten A&M twice earlier in the season, the Aggies caught fire. A&M beat TCU, 8-1, and won its next five SWC games to set up a two-game showdown with Texas at rickety ol' Kyle Field, which backed up to the west stands of the Aggies' home football stadium. Earlier in the season, Texas had hammered out a 14-10 win over A&M in Austin, and the Aggies needed to beat UT in back-to-back games in College Station in order to claim a tie for the SWC crown.

The Longhorns were a pressure-tested bunch, as UT had won national championships in 1949 and '50—the first two years the College World Series was played in Omaha's Rosenblatt Stadium. Texas was so confident that it would win at least one game in College Station that Falk announced he would waive all NCAA rights, including a possible one-game playoff between A&M and Texas, if the Aggies swept the series.

Behind the pitching of Pat Hubert, the Aggies beat the Longhorns 4-2 on May 17 to set up a winner-take-all showdown the following day. With another stellar pitching performance from Bob Tankersley, the Aggies hammered out a 4-1 win that propelled A&M into a best-of-three playoff series at Arizona.

It would prove to be one of the most uplifting series in A&M baseball history. But Ogletree recalls that it began with one of the most terrifying flights of his life.

"It was a white-knuckle flight for a lot us, and it was probably the first time to fly for some of us," Ogletree said. "The plane was real old and full of flies. It was hot, too. We ran through a rain storm and didn't know if we were going to make it or not. It certainly wasn't first class.

Then, when we got to Tucson, we found out we weren't even staying in a motel. We stayed in the equipment room under the football stadium. In the latter part of May, it's awfully hot in Arizona. It was a wide-open space that wasn't even enclosed. They just threw a bunch of army cots in there for us to sleep on. We also had to walk half a mile to the cafeteria to eat."

But R.C. "Beau" Bell, who had replaced Karow as the Aggies' head coach prior to the 1951 season, reminded his players they had come to Tucson to play ball, not to vacation. And before a crowd of 1,200 fans at Arizona's University Diamond on May 23, the Aggies trailed 4-3 heading into the ninth inning. Yale Lary opened the Aggies' ninth with a single and was at third with two outs when Henry "Yogi" Candelari popped the ball up in the infield. Arizona shortstop Ron Nicely circled under it to apparently record the final out of the game, and fans were literally leaving the stadium as the ball hit Nicely's glove. But before he could secure it, the ball popped out. Lary trotted home with the tying run and Candelari ended up at second on the error. The next A&M batter was Ogletree, who laced a double into the gap to score Candelari with what proved to be the game-winning run.

Arizona pummeled the Aggies, 21-4, in the second game, but A&M jumped to a 9-0 lead in the third game and coasted to a 14-2 win. For the first time ever, the Aggies were bound for Omaha.

"That's where everyone wanted to go," Ogletree said. "We knew it was a big deal, but I'm not sure anyone really knew how big of a deal it was. The College World Series wasn't very old; it was fairly new to everyone. The only thing we knew was that Texas had won it the year before, and we wanted to top Texas."

A&M did not top Texas's feat, as the Aggies were knocked out of the double-elimination tournament in three games. Ironically, the only win for the Aggies in Omaha came against an Ohio State team coached by Karow, who left Aggieland for Columbus following the 1950 season.

But simply making it to the CWS was a remarkable accomplishment—a feat Ogletree would later duplicate as a coach. After his playing days ended at A&M, Ogletree played several minor league seasons in Texas and in Louisiana. Following the 1955 season, Ogletree was offered a fellowship by the head of the PE department at A&M to come back to College Station to earn his master's degree. With a wife and two kids, Ogletree figured the time was now or never to work toward his dreams of coaching.

"We went back to A&M and stayed at College View Apartments, which were like army barracks," Ogletree said. "The rent was $30 a month with all bills paid. I taught seven classes in the physical education department, which gave me $25 per class a month, and I was also on the G.I. Bill. I thought I was in high cotton."

Ogletree finished his master's in 1956 and was told by Burger about a new athletic program at the University of Dallas, a tiny Catholic college in Irving. When he accepted the job in Dallas, the school's total enrollment was just under 100 students. Only 15 of the students were male.

"Twelve of the boys played baseball," Ogletree said. "A couple of them had never played before, but we recruited them so we'd have enough. I had nine that played basketball. When we played intrasquad games, I had to play on one side to give us 10. I coached everything—basketball, baseball and I had one track man and one golfer. I taught seven PE classes, and I was the bookstore manager, too."

In the early years at Dallas, Ogletree played high school teams, military bases and anyone else he could schedule. It took him four years to win his first game, as Dallas beat Austin College for career victory No. 1. "When I was 0-22, I started to wonder whether I was in the right profession," he said with a laugh.

Ogletree stayed in Dallas for nine years before leaving for Sul Ross State University, where he was the head baseball coach and assistant football coach. In his third year in Alpine, Ogletree guided Sul Ross to the NAIA World Series. But on the trip home from Missouri, he and his team learned the university decided to drop the baseball program. Ogletree, however, wasn't out of baseball for long. He received a call from Pan American athletic director James Brooks, who offered him the head coaching position in Edinburg, just a few miles north of the Mexican border. Ogletree leapt at the opportunity, taking one of his best players, Reggie Tredaway, with him.

Ogletree won 24 games his first season and led Pan American to the NCAA playoffs in his second year. In his third season, Pan American swept the Longhorns in the NCAA playoffs to reach the CWS.

"Getting to the College World Series as a coach was really special," Ogletree said. "It was exactly 20 years after we made it at A&M, and I saw Marty Karow in Omaha. That was probably the highlight of my coaching career, but we had a lot of great seasons."

In '75, he won 63 games, and in 1983, he led Pan American to 64 wins. If not for running into a couple of UT pitchers named Roger Clemens and Calvin Shiraldi in the '83 regional tournament in Austin, Pan American may have made a second CWS.

After 41 years of coaching and 44 years of teaching—44 was also his jersey number—Ogletree decided to turn things over to assistant coach Reggie Tredaway, the player he had brought with him from Sul Ross in the late 1960s. Ogletree ended his career in 1997 with 1,217 victories, and the pitcher who earned his 1,200th victory happened to be Marty Karow's great-grandson. Even more ironically, he won it against Notre Dame, the school he once dreamed about attending.

"I had such a blessed career, and I met so many great people along the way," said the 74-year-old Ogletree, who still resides in McAllen with his wife of 50 years, Joann. "I have five kids, 11 grandchildren and a great-grandson. Aside from my family, baseball's been my life, and I am so lucky to have been around the game for as long as I was. It's been my passion, my love. My wife said one time, if she'd put some bases in the yard, I might have taken care of that. I've really been blessed every step along the way, starting with some good advice to go to Texas A&M."

JOHN BEASLEY

Dirk Nowitzki. Michael Finley. Steve Nash. Mark Aguirre. Rolando Blackman. Brad Davis. John Beasley.

John Beasley?

Most Dallas basketball fans can tell you that the first six names on that list constitute the greatest names in the history of Dallas Mavericks basketball. But the greybeards of the Metroplex group will also attest that the seventh name certainly belongs on any list of the greatest players ever to play professional basketball in "Big D."

In fact, the well-versed Dallas basketball fans will also point out that the last player on that list may have been the most prominent. Beasley is the only player in Dallas basketball pro history to win MVP honors for an All-Star game, and although it takes some tooth-pulling techniques to convince him to talk about it today, Beasley was probably the first great professional basketball player in Dallas.

He is certainly the most successful professional basketball player to ever come out of Texas A&M, and he is the only Aggie to ever make an All-Star game appearance. The humble, down-home Beasley played in three American Basketball Association All-Star Games, winning the MVP in 1969.

Photo courtesy of Texas A&M Athletic Media Relations

JOHN BEASLEY
A&M Letterman: 1964-66

Sport: Basketball
Position: Forward
First-team All-American: 1966
Two-time SWC Player of the Year
Still owns school's career records for scoring (21.8)
and rebounding (10.8) averages

"I would say the opportunity to play in the All-Star Games was more of a highlight to me than the honor of winning MVP," said Beasley, one of only two first-team All-Americans in Aggie basketball history. "Winning the MVP is just a matter of whoever kind of gets hot that night. In the All-Star Game, everybody shoots, and I just happened to be hot that night."

Beasley, who was formerly a longtime salesman with Converse and is now the North Texas account manager for a safety equipment company, was hot on most nights during his highly productive and successful career on the hardwood. In his first three seasons with the ABA's Dallas Chaparrals, Beasley averaged 19.1 points and 11.8 rebounds.

Beasley played four and a half seasons with the Chaparrals, who went on to become the San Antonio Spurs, and he finished his pro career with three seasons in Utah. The six-foot-nine Beasley also played in the first-ever ABA-NBA game, going toe to toe against the Milwaukee Bucks and their star center Lew Alcindor, who would later change his name to Kareem Abdul-Jabbar.

"I remember they won, but that game came right down to the wire," said Beasley, who now lives near Athens, Texas on Cedar Creek Lake. "The ABA was really good. At that point, we had players like Julius Erving, Moses Malone, David Thompson, Dan Issel and Artis Gilmore coming into the ABA because the money was better [than in the NBA]. That's what started the bidding war. Eventually it forced the merger between the two leagues. But there was some awfully good basketball being played in the ABA."

For all of his ABA heroics, however, Beasley is most proud of his accomplishments and association with his alma mater. Growing up in far Northeast Texas, Beasley had little knowledge of and no ties to Texas A&M. But he was impressed that former A&M coach Bob Rogers was willing to make the drive from College Station to Kildare, which is located about halfway between Longview and Texarkana, on a weekly basis just to visit with him. And once Beasley visited A&M for himself, he quickly fell in love with Aggieland.

"Bob Rogers came to see me every Wednesday for most of the year," Beasley said. "I got close to him, and then I visited Texas A&M and went to a football game. The spirit and the tradition sold me almost immediately. I was coming from little ol' Linden-Kildare High School, and when I saw all of the spirit and traditions of A&M, I knew it was the right place for me. Then when I got down there, I was even more impressed. Back when I played, the gym was packed, the band came and played loud, and it was a happening. I guess I was so impressed with what was happening all around me that it kind of took my freshman and sophomore year to really understand what I needed to do on the basketball floor."

Once Beasley figured it out, he was practically unstoppable. He was solid as a sophomore, averaging 12.3 points and 9.5 rebounds as the Aggies won the 1964 Southwest Conference championship in Shelby Metcalf's first season as head coach. It was in his final two seasons, however, when Beasley etched his name permanently in the Texas A&M and SWC record books.

Beasley led the SWC in scoring in 1965 by averaging 28.6 points per game in league competition. And in '66, he was even better, pouring in an amazing 30.6 points per contest in SWC play. Beasley was named the SWC Player of the Year in 1965 and again in '66. He is also the last Texas A&M basketball player to be selected as a first-team All-American, capturing the honor as a senior in 1966.

Beasley still owns a number of Texas A&M records, including career rebounding average (10.8) and career scoring average (21.8). He is also the No. 3 scorer in A&M history with 1,594 points in his three-year varsity career.

"I was blessed to have had a good career and I was very fortunate to have played it at Texas A&M," said Beasley, the father of one grown daughter and two sons who are now in the basketball coaching profession. "I wouldn't have gone to any other school. To me, it's such a fine school. I don't know where you would ever go to have the spirit, tradition and camaraderie that our school has. I've played on college campuses all over the country, and I've played in pro arenas. It's not the same as Texas A&M.

"Honestly, I think we've lost some of that atmosphere in recent years in our basketball program, but no matter what our record is this year or any other year, I'm very proud of being a part of Texas A&M basketball history. In fact, I'd say the best basketball honor I've ever received was to be named to the all-time Texas A&M and Southwest Conference teams a few years back. Those were big honors to me."

Beasley was honored again by his alma mater on January 11, 2003 at halftime of an A&M game at Reed Arena. He and the other three surviving A&M players who had earned first-, second- or third-team All-America status (Walter Davis, Carroll Broussard and Bennie Lenox) were introduced to the crowd, while the deceased Jewell McDowell was also recognized. Beasley, who was originally drafted by the NBA's Baltimore Bullets in 1966, says he was thrilled to be recognized once again in

John Beasley (far left) is honored at Reed Arena during the 2002-03 season along with other former A&M All-Americans. Beasley was a first-team All-American in 1966 and was the two-time SWC Player of the Year. (Photo courtesy of Texas A&M Athletic Media Relations)

Aggieland. But mostly, he says, he was just pleased to be back in his element.

"I had so many great times and have such fond memories of my days playing basketball at Texas A&M, and I would love to see us get back to that kind of competitive level in the Big 12. And I'd love to see the Aggie fans and the folks in the community really get behind the team like they did back when I played."

Perhaps that will eventually happen, but it will probably first take the Aggies landing a few more players like John Beasley to ignite the crowd and the community.

CURTIS MILLS

It was the first week on the Texas A&M campus for freshman sprinter Curtis Mills, and when he heard the late-night knock on his dorm room door, Mills opened it to find a small, burning cross.

Mills, the first African-American athlete ever to be awarded a scholarship at Texas A&M, anticipated some strange looks and was prepared for some muffled slurs behind his back, but he didn't know what to make of this.

"That first night in September of 1967, I really just kind of took it as a joke or some kind of initiation thing," said Mills, now a supervisor for Travis County's Transportation and Natural Resources Department. "But then it happened a second night, a third night and a fourth night. I began thinking they didn't want us to go here."

Mills and two other African-American athletes then met with A&M coaches. A meeting was held, a mandate was issued. Nothing similar ever happened again. In fact, Mills now jokes that, from that point forward, he practically had to beg fellow athletes and classmates to be treated just as badly as the rest of the underclassmen.

"We just wanted to fit in, to be Aggies," Mills said. "If there was an initiation, we said, 'Give it to us.' But everybody was being so polite. At one point, they would ask us if it was OK to initiate us. I said, 'You

Photo courtesy of Texas A&M Athletic Media Relations

CURTIS MILLS
A&M Letterman: 1968-71

Sport: Track and Field
Position: Sprinter
1969 NCAA champion and world record setter
in the 440-yard dash (44.7)
1969 and '70 All-American in the 440 and 440 relay
Three consecutive SWC titles in the 440

don't ask the other freshmen. Don't ask us. Just do it.' So they took us all out—the white guys, the black guys, all of us—and sprayed us with paint, dumped us out in the country and told us to find our way back to campus. They don't do that any more, of course. But it was great. It wasn't about skin color. It was about being an Aggie. I was proud to be an Aggie then, and I'm still just as proud to be an Aggie now."

In the big picture of things, Mills is definitely one of the all-time great Aggie athletes. And whether he was breaking racial barriers or track and field records, Mills has always made it clear that the color he most likes to be defined by is maroon. That hasn't changed. Mills is a regular at Aggie athletic events throughout the year—at home or away.

He takes a great deal of pride in being a pioneer at A&M for future African-American athletes and students. But most of all, he swells with pride regarding how the students at A&M in the late 1960s welcomed him and made him part of the Aggie family. The isolated incidents during his first week on campus may have been an example of the racial unrest that permeated much of the South during that era. But how he was treated over the next four years was an example of the spirit and camaraderie that has long set Texas A&M apart from other universities.

"I'm from Lufkin, and I went to Dunbar High School before integration," Mills said. "It was an all-black school, and I figured I was heading to an all-black university, probably Southern University. But it ended up that I came to Texas A&M, and I am so thankful that I did. I don't know about how other African-Americans felt about racial issues at that time, but it wasn't a barrier at Texas A&M. In the process of learning how to 'hump it' and do the yells and learn all the other traditions, I just felt like an Aggie. Not a black Aggie. You don't have time to worry about who has what or how rich or poor you are, or whether you're white or black. I just wanted to be an Aggie, and those students wanted me to be an Aggie."

Once he learned the university's traditions, Mills began working on carrying on the tradition of A&M's track and field excellence. Three-time NCAA shot-put champion and future Olympic gold medalist Randy Matson was finishing up at A&M just as Mills was arriving. But Mills immediately went to work on keeping Aggie track and field in the national spotlight.

By the time he was done at A&M, Mills had set or been part of 11 school records. He also won seven Southwest Conference titles and won the 1969 national title with a then world record time of 44.7 second in the 440-yard dash. En route to setting the world record in '69, Mills shocked the crowd in Knoxville, Tennessee by beating 1968 gold medalist Lee Evans and silver winner Larry James.

Mills, a three-time All-American at A&M, also teamed with his younger brother, Marvin, to set two world records in 1970. The quartet of Harold McMahan, Willie Blackmon and the Mills brothers set the indoor mile record (3:05.7) in Houston. Then Donny Rogers, Rockie Woods and the Mills brothers set the 880-yard relay record (1:21.7) in Des Moines.

Mills didn't put Texas A&M track and field on the map, but he made it a much more desirable destination for future standouts.

"I had never been to A&M when I was in high school, and I didn't know anyone who went to A&M," Mills said. "But when I visited, I thought it was great, and I thought it was a great opportunity to be the first black athlete to sign a scholarship to go to A&M. 'Howdy' wasn't a part of anything I said before I went there. But before long, we were hollering 'howdy.' I knew then that me and the other black athletes I came in with were going to fit in. And in terms of track, I just knew we were going to win and do something very special. And it wasn't just the individual stuff that mattered to me. It was the team. We wanted to win it as a team."

With Mills leading the way, that's exactly what the Aggies did in 1970. A&M ended a 16-year drought to give Charlie Thomas his first SWC outdoor title. Mills won the 220, the 440 and anchored the title-winning 440-yard relay team.

"At the time, I never thought about how rewarding winning that team title was," Mills said. "We were young, just competing and trying to take A&M to the top. Now, when I look back on it, I realize that we were pretty good. What's funny is that it all came back to me in 2001 when we won the Big 12 championship there in College Station. I was there, and I was giving out awards. I'm not sure how those current athletes felt about winning the championship, but that was pretty special for me to see. It just brought back a lot of great memories and gave me a lot of pride to have been associated with Texas A&M track and field."

Mills, who received a degree in education from A&M, felt a similar amount of pride when he was inducted into the Texas A&M Athletic Hall of Fame in 1970 and again when the Texas A&M Sports Museum was officially opened in the summer of '01. Mills is prominently featured in The Legends Gallery.

"That was beyond my wildest imagination," Mills said of the recognition in the museum. "I'm really honored."

*Curtis Mills, who now lives in the Austin area, enjoys a big laugh inside the
A&M Sports Museum as he views a huge photo of him in his prime physical condition at A&M.* (Photo courtesy of the Texas A&M Athletic Sports Museum)

When Mills left A&M, he went north and ran for the Philadelphia Track Club for five years, while also beginning a career in teaching. He then returned to Texas, working a couple years for the Waco Parks and Recreation Department and then for the next eight years as a highway patrolman.

In 1986, he settled in Travis County and has been there ever since. He provides a variety of services for the Transportation and Natural Resources Department, and as a supervisor, Mills makes certain that all of his employees are constantly reminded where his heart can always be found.

"It's a fun job, because every day is different," said Mills, who celebrated his 18th anniversary with the department in 2004. "We work with other departments, we have inmate programs, work with the senior citizens and provide just a wide variety of services. And we have a good group of employees, although being in Travis County, I deal with a lot of Longhorns all the time. But they all know I bleed maroon, and I'm never afraid to remind them of that fact."

DOUG RAU

Throughout his life, Doug Rau has often possessed an uncanny sixth sense for first impressions. It's a Rau talent that comes in handy today as the co-owner of Crown Financial, LLC, a short-term, assets-based lending company in the Houston area. It's also a gift that has shaped his life in many ways.

Rau usually knows exactly what he likes when he sees it. No over-analyzing, no second-guessing. Rau simply goes for it. That explains why he is happily married to a woman he met in the first grade. That also explains why the country boy from outside of tiny Columbus, Texas, originally chose Texas A&M over a much more heralded University of Texas baseball program.

"I was drafted way down the line out of high school by Baltimore," Rau said. "But my mind was pretty much made up that, unless the Orioles offered a lot of money, I was going to play for Coach [Tom] Chandler at A&M. That decision was relatively easy for me. I did visit Texas, but there was something special in Tom Chandler's personality that made me go in that direction. I just had a good feeling about him right from the start."

Rau's first impression about Chandler eventually helped him to become a first-round draft pick of the Los Angeles Dodgers, where Rau

Photo courtesy of Texas A&M Athletic Media Relations

DOUG RAU
A&M Letterman: 1968-70

Sport: Baseball
Position: Pitcher
Career collegiate ERA of 1.51 (lowest in school history)
1970 All-America Pitcher with 0.86 ERA
1970 first-round draft pick of the Los Angeles Dodgers
Two World Series Appearances (1977 and '78)

played for legendary managers such as Tom Lasorda and Gene Mauch, pitched in the same rotation with Hall of Famers Tommy John and Don Sutton, and played in two memorable World Series against the New York Yankees. But of all the moments and men he recalls in a lifetime full of baseball memories, Rau says no one influenced his career like the late Tom Chandler. The former Texas A&M head coach did more to transform Rau into a polished pitcher than anybody else he encountered.

"The greatest influence on my life as a baseball player was Tom Chandler and still is Tom Chandler," said Rau, a six-foot-two lefty who arrived on the A&M campus in 1967. "After you've been out of the game, you look back and ask, 'Who really had the greatest influence on me as a player?' I could say my dad, I could say Tommy Lasorda, and I could say my high school coach. But when you get right down to it, I'm certain it was Tom Chandler. In terms of the formative years, learning how to handle myself mentally and physically and developing as a complete player, Coach Chandler was the man."

Under Chandler's tutelage, Rau won All-Southwest Conference honors as a freshman in '68 and was a first-team All-American as a junior in '70 when Rau compiled a school-record 0.86 ERA. In his three seasons at A&M, the Aggies went 61-27, and Rau was as dominant a starting pitcher as Texas A&M fans had ever seen. His miniscule career earned run average at A&M (1.51) still ranks as the best in school history.

Rau says he never dreamed of performing so well at the collegiate level. But he spent most of his life dreaming of reaching the next level. Growing up along Farm Road 109, Rau and his younger brother spent much of their time working the hay meadows, the watermelon patches and the local service station. But whenever there was extra time on his hands, Rau usually had a baseball in his left hand. And from the time he can remember, the small-town boy had big-league dreams. He received his shot at "the show" following his spectacular junior season at A&M.

"I signed in the spring of 1970," Rau said. "That was when the Vietnam War was heating up, and I nervously went to the library one night knowing that the lottery was going to be picked that night. Three hours later, I learned my number was 320, and I could go into pro ball with no worries about having to fight overseas. So with my mind relieved, I began my pro career in 1970."

That's also when he stepped onto the fast track to the big leagues. He had given himself only a two- or three-year window to make it into major league baseball. If he hadn't made it during that time frame, he planned to finish his degree at A&M and begin graduate studies. But

Rau surprised even himself with how quickly he made it to the majors. He made major strides playing winter ball in 1971, and by August of 1972, he was called up to join the big-league roster. Rau's debut in Dodger blue came on September 2, 1972, at Busch Stadium in St. Louis. He'll never forget the first batter he faced.

"The first hitter was Lou Brock," recalled Rau, who turned 55 in 2003. "He grounded to short on the second pitch, and I said to myself, 'I may be able to handle this excitement.' We won the game, and I pitched a couple times in relief later that year. I knew that if I went to winter ball a couple more times I would have a chance to rejoin the big -league team. Going with [former Dodgers vice president] Al Campanis's and Tommy Lasorda's plan of stressing the importance of playing in South America or the Dominican Republic, I developed in terms of character and ability. The following two winters, in '72 and '73, I spent half-seasons in Santa Domingo with Lasorda again as the manager. I thought the winter of '72 is where I turned a corner to make me a bona fide major league pitcher."

Rau went 4-2 with the Dodgers in '73 and then began an exceptional five-year string in '74, where he averaged over 14 wins per season from 1974-78. Pitching on the same staff that included John, Sutton, Burt Hooton, Rick Rhoden and Charlie Hough, Rau compiled 73 wins during that stretch and helped lead the Dodgers to back-to-back World Series appearances in '77 and '78.

"I learned to pitch, and I had a great bunch of guys to play with," Rau said. "But about the time I had the routine down is when I ran into problems with a shoulder injury in '79. I fought that for a long time both physically and mentally. But I had a good run. It certainly wasn't anything too special to a guy just looking at numbers. But there were times when I thought I could get anybody in baseball out. It gives me some pride and gives me something to sleep on every night that I at least made it [to the majors] and hung in there for a while."

Rau underwent shoulder surgery in June of 1979 and was prepared to make a return to the Dodgers in 1981. But just days before he reported to spring training, the Dodgers released him. He eventually signed with the California Angels that summer, but he never returned to his mid-1970s form.

After leaving the game for good, Rau eventually returned to the Lone Star State following the birth of his daughter, Stephanie. While searching for the business opportunity that felt right, Rau helped his brother begin a petroleum business and also began investing in a handful of real estate partnerships in the Houston area. Throughout his search

Doug Rau, an All-America pitcher for the Aggies in 1970, is now the co-owner of Crown Financial LLC, in Houston. He and his wife, Rhonda, are usually in the stands at the ballpark in Aggieland with their daughter, Stephanie, a student at A&M. (Photo courtesy of Doug Rau)

for the perfect profession, Rau spent plenty of time at the ballpark, working with kids in the Houston area who—like he had long before—shared the dream of making it big in baseball. In fact, it was through baseball that Rau met his future business partner.

"I was doing a variety of things, but mainly, I was waiting for some opportunity that made sense," Rau said. "I had thought about going back into baseball and was spending free time working with kids. That led me to my business partner right now, who has three young pitchers that all went on to become quite successful in college and even two of them in pro careers. I just kind of followed the path of least resistance and ended up at Crown Financial."

In a sense, Rau is still pitching. But now, he is working to make connections instead of Ks. Crown Financial, LLC, which was formed in '99, specializes in bridge loans to small businesses and individuals that may take a client from one level to the next faster and more efficiently than banks can perform. And as the co-owner of the company, Rau has the flexibility to enjoy the loves of his life—family and baseball at Texas A&M. Rau is now a frequent visitor at Olsen Field, where he and his wife mix visits with their daughter, who is a student at A&M, with one of the most prominent influences of their life: Aggie baseball.

"I've been very blessed to have some wonderful people in my life," Rau said. "My wife, Rhonda, and I met in the first grade. We were married in 1974, and I've had one girlfriend in all my years of existence. I feel very blessed about that. I also have a wonderful daughter, Stephanie, and I'm so delighted she is now a student at A&M. And while there have been many special bonds that I've made in baseball, I'll always look back at the bond I had with Coach Chandler with the most special memories. He was a true mentor, a true friend and truly one of the finest men I met in baseball. The relationship I had with him really helped to shape my life, and I'll always be grateful to him."

SONNY PARKER

During a career at Texas A&M that spanned more than three decades as an assistant and head coach, Shelby Metcalf coached hundreds of players, recruited thousands and can readily recall hundreds of thousands of memorable moments. So when the witty, engaging Metcalf begins a nostalgic stroll down memory lane, pull up a chair and make yourself comfortable. You're going to be here awhile.

The greatest games? Metcalf has a long list of them. The greatest seasons? He has several favorites. But when the subject of his greatest player arises, it's somewhat surprising that Metcalf delivers a definitive answer as quickly as Michael Jordan's first step.

"Sonny Parker. He's the most talented player we ever had at A&M," said Metcalf, the head coach of the Aggies from 1963-90. "And I've never seen a player with that much talent work so hard. Sonny was really incredibly talented. We used to joke when watching the tape the day after a game that we needed to put it on slow motion, because he was so quick he just looked like a blur at regular speed. He was always on the move."

He still is. The Chicago native is back in the Windy City, moving, shaking and utilizing basketball to help others. As the creator, director and namesake of the Sonny Parker Youth Foundation, since 1990 Parker

Photo courtesy of Texas A&M Athletic Media Relations

SONNY PARKER
A&M Letterman: 1975-76

Sport: Basketball
Position: Guard/Forward
First-team All-SWC 1975 and '76
SWC Player of the Year 1975 and '76
First-round draft pick of Golden State Warriors 1976

has worked with thousands of inner-city and disadvantaged kids in Chicago, using basketball as a tool to teach life's lessons.

Parker has also worked previously for the Jordan Boys and Girls Club in Chicago, named after Michael Jordan's father. But no matter where he has been employed in his post-basketball playing career, the theme of Parker's work has always been the same: helping kids. Considering that he is the proud father of seven children of his own, it could also be considered the theme of Parker's life.

"It's very rewarding to still be involved with basketball and to be able to make a difference in the lives of these kids," said Parker, who led the Aggies to back-to-back Southwest Conference titles in the mid-1970s. "These kids are our future, and we feel like we are making a difference in the future by the work we are doing. We use basketball as a vehicle, and we continually preach that we don't allow basketball to use us. We also check on their grades to keep up with their progress.

"I mentor a lot of the kids personally, so I have a one-on-one relationship with them. We have a basketball academy where we teach, train and develop kids from ages five to 14. I also have five traveling teams as well as an AAU team. But our fundamental purpose is more about making a difference than making baskets."

Parker has enjoyed plenty of success in both areas. In addition to serving as a positive role model for countless Chicago kids, Parker has helped to nurture and develop the talents of some of the biggest names in basketball. Through his summer camps, Parker has worked NBA stars such as Michael Finley, Tim Hardaway, Glenn Robinson and Kevin Garnett.

Parker has an ability to reach kids with NBA visions because he's excelled on that level. Parker is still the last A&M player to make a significant impact in the NBA, as he spent six seasons with the Golden State Warriors, averaging double figures in three of those seasons and near double figures for his career. He played on some great teams at Golden State and played with some of the NBA's best players in that era, including Rick Barry, Robert Parish, World B. Free and Bernard King.

Throughout all of his basketball successes and accomplishments at various levels, Parker says one of the most meaningful honors he has ever received was being inducted in 2000 into the A&M Athletic Hall of Fame. A junior college transfer, Parker only spent two years at A&M, and before the induction ceremony, he had not been back to College Station in a dozen years.

But Parker has always beamed with maroon pride at the mere mention of Texas A&M. He considered it an honor to carry the Aggie flag in the NBA. And he finds it difficult to put into words just how much it meant to him to be recognized by his alma mater.

"It was hard to describe," said Parker. "I was really excited about it and really appreciative. I think that honor meant so much to me because it went beyond just my basketball skills. They looked at my character. There are many great players who have come and gone at A&M, and I think that they looked at a lot of the things I've done in representing A&M. I've always been so proud to be an Aggie."

Aggie fans have certainly always been proud to call Parker one of their own. Parker led the Aggies to the NCAA Tournament in 1974-75, averaged 20.7 points per game as a senior in 1975-76 and was a first-team All-SWC performer both years. Only two A&M players have averaged at least 20 points per game since Parker departed.

While Parker doesn't have many opportunities to return to Texas A&M, he says he certainly uses his Aggie experiences in the messages he delivers to his kids.

"We had a meeting recently with some of the kids I work with, some seventh and eighth graders, and I was just telling them how important it is to seek their education first," Parker said. "We've had a lot of top players here, and we always preach, 'no books, no ball.' And I tell them about how just getting to go to a great college like Texas A&M laid the foundation for so many things for me. It's a lesson I really try to get into their heads."

It's a message his own children have obviously received. Parker's oldest son is a graduate of the University of Oregon and now works with his father in the youth foundation. He has another daughter who recently graduated from college, and the four youngest children, who live at home, are already formulating their college plans. And for 16-year-old Christian Parker, those college plans could include Texas A&M.

Christian Parker came to his father's induction ceremony at Texas A&M as a big-time Duke fan. By the time the weekend was over, however, Sonny's son acknowledged his visit had been an allegiance-altering experience, as he fully embraced the Spirit of Aggieland and subsequently renounced the Devils of Blue.

"He came with all his Duke stuff and left with a suitcase full of maroon," said Christian's mother and Sonny's wife, Lola Parker. "Chris has been to universities all over the country, and like most teenagers, he's a very independent thinker. Sonny told him before what a neat place Texas A&M was, but he wasn't buying into it. Then he experienced Texas A&M for himself. He couldn't believe how sincere and genuine the people were. He couldn't believe the spirit. He said as we were leaving that

A Chicago native, Sonny Parker is back in the Windy City these days. He is the creator, director and namesake of the Sonny Parker Youth Foundation. Since 1990, Parker has worked with thousands of inner-city and disadvantaged kids in Chicago, using basketball as a tool to teach life's lessons. (Photo courtesy of Texas A&M Athletic Sports Museum)

this is where he wanted to go to school. He said, 'Mom, I'm an Aggie. This place is incredible.' It thrilled his father that Texas A&M had made such an impression on him."

That's only one of the things that made the induction ceremony so special to Sonny Parker. Even with part of his family on hand, Parker never envisioned just how emotionally moving the event would be. During the ceremony, Metcalf presented a watch to Christian Parker. It was the same watch that Sonny Parker had given to Metcalf 25 years earlier.

"Sonny had been the MVP of a senior All-Star game, and he had been given a watch with the inscription 'Sonny P, MVP' on it," Metcalf said. "Sonny had 'To Coach Metcalf' inscribed on it, as well. It had meant a lot to me that he did that, and that's why I kept it for 25 years. But I told him now that I'm such an old man that time just gets in my way. So I wanted his son to have it back."

A teary-eyed Sonny Parker said that he was quite moved by Metcalf's gesture.

"Coach Metcalf and Mrs. Metcalf have always been like family to me," Parker said. "And to see Coach Metcalf present that to my son, I was just taken a little bit emotionally because he's been so much to me and developed me not only as a basketball player, but also as a person. He taught me about building character. Then to share that experience and to get the watch back over some 25 years, it just made me so thankful to be a part of the Aggie family. Texas A&M was a perfect fit for me more than 25 years ago, and it was really neat to see that Chris saw it may be the place for him, too. Texas A&M has changed so much since I was there going to school, but it's still the greatest place to me."

Likewise, Sonny Parker may still be the greatest basketball player to ever wear the Aggies' maroon and white. At least according to Metcalf, there's no doubt about it.

MARK
THURMOND

Shortly after departing Texas A&M in the summer of 1979, a rather weary and wavering Mark Thurmond vividly recalls looking out the window of his Amarillo apartment, staring at the wind-whipped, horizontal flags and pondering two things: Would the gale-force gusts in the Panhandle ever die down? And would his earned run average ever go down?

"I was getting beat up in the minor leagues and asking myself how in the world I thought I was going to get Mike Schmidt and Pete Rose and guys like that out," Thurmond recalled. "If I couldn't get minor league hitters out, how was I going to make it in the majors? I wasn't giving up, but I wasn't making long-term plans [in baseball], either. I had doubts."

Fortunately, Thurmond also had drive. Just a few years after making his shaky debut in the Texas League, the left-hander was mowing down the best of the best in the big leagues. In 1984, Thurmond was a National League All-Star in the summer, and he was the Game 1 starter for the San Diego Padres in the World Series that fall. He obviously figured out how to handle Schmidt, Rose and the rest of the best hitters in baseball. He also made a rather startling realization while rising to the top of his profession.

Photo courtesy of Texas A&M Athletic Media Relations

MARK THURMOND
A&M Letterman: 1976-79

Sport: Baseball
Position: Pitcher
Two-time All-America Pitcher: 1977 and '78
First-team All-SWC in 1977 and '78
3.69 career ERA in eight seasons in the Major Leagues
1984 All-Star and Game 1 starter in the 1984 World Series

"As strange as this sounds, it was actually easier to pitch in the major leagues than it was in AA," said Thurmond, a two-time All-American at A&M. "I got to the major leagues, and I realized they have better fields, better fielders, better lights. In Amarillo, the lights were so bad that outfielders would lose routine fly balls that turned into doubles and triples. That was tough on your ERA. Pitching in Amarillo made me better. You better learn to pitch quickly there because the wind blew straight out, and the ball flew because it was a higher altitude. I had to learn to pitch quickly or I wouldn't have been pitching very long."

Thurmond pitched longer in the big leagues than he at one time envisioned, spending more than eight years in "the show." During his major league career, which featured stints with the Padres, Tigers, Orioles and Giants, Thurmond made 97 starts, appeared in 314 games and amassed an impressive career ERA of 3.69. There were numerous memorable moments during his big league career, but perhaps the most unforgettable day occurred on October 8, 1984 at Jack Murphy Stadium.

After compiling a 14-8 record in the regular season with a sparkling 2.97 ERA, Thurmond earned the Game 1 start in the World Series, matching up against Detroit Tigers ace Jack Morris. Before Thurmond ever toed the rubber that evening, he experienced a magical moment, swelling with maroon pride as Pat Olsen tossed out the ceremonial first pitch.

Olsen—the namesake for Olsen Field—attended 279 consecutive World Series games during his lifetime. Olsen fired a strike and then Thurmond went to work, becoming a part of Aggie trivia forever.

Q: Who are the two Aggies who threw the first pitch in the 1984 World Series?

For Thurmond, however, the warm, fuzzy feelings quickly dispersed. Facing a Detroit lineup that featured stars like Lance Parrish, Darrell Evans, Alan Trammell, Lou Whitaker and the volatile Kirk Gibson, Thurmond went to battle in what he now calls the most difficult pitching assignment of his life.

"It had nothing to do with the pressure of starting the first game of the World Series," Thurmond said of the game, which has appeared on ESPN's Classic Sports. "The Tigers were so good at fouling off pitches they couldn't handle until they could get something they could handle. It was real frustrating. You'd make the pitch you wanted with two strikes, they'd foul it off, then you'd go two-two [in the count], and they'd foul two more off. The count would be three-two, and by that time, I'd thrown nine pitches. I always tried to get a batter out in five pitches or less. I pitched complete games in the big leagues throwing 95 to 101 pitches. But in that game, I had 116 [pitches] in five innings. It was a tough night."

In a valiant and gutsy effort, Thurmond was eventually tagged with a 3-2 loss, and the Padres, making their first-ever World Series appearance, were beaten in five games. Despite the bittersweet memories, Thurmond remains extremely grateful for the opportunity to perform on baseball's biggest stage. But when he begins recounting his baseball blessings, Thurmond starts with his days at A&M.

Thurmond arrived at A&M in the fall of 1975 with some large shoes to fill. His older brother, Al, was a two-sport standout in Aggieland from 1973-75, playing safety for Emory Bellard and earning All-SWC honors as an outfielder for Tom Chandler. Mark initially planned on following in his brother's two-sport footsteps, signing with Bellard as a talented quarterback prospect from Houston Spring Branch. But while he was playing in the outfield during a summer league game, Thurmond began thinking about his long-term future. His football career would probably never go past the collegiate level, but if he devoted his time to baseball, Thurmond believed he could make a pro career on the diamond. So a few weeks before two-a-day football practices began, Thurmond placed a call.

"I called [Bellard] and told him," Thurmond said. "He respected my decision. But I was on a football scholarship the first year because I'd already signed the scholarship; then I was transferred to a baseball scholarship my sophomore year. Maybe that's another trivia question I'm part of. 'What player never played football who was on a full football scholarship?'"

Thurmond's baseball-only focus proved to be a wise decision. He started in the outfield as a freshman and entered practices the following year as the No. 4 pitcher in Chandler's rotation. During the second SWC series of the 1977 season, Thurmond earned his first start and promptly pitched a shutout. The rest is record-book history. Teaming with Mark Ross at the top of the rotation, Thurmond helped lead the Aggies to back-to-back SWC titles in 1977 and '78. Thurmond earned All-America honors both seasons, and his name is still highlighted numerous times in the A&M record books.

During his brilliant collegiate career, Thurmond posted 34 wins (tied for the most in school history), tossed a school-record 11 shutouts and pitched 25 complete games (second most in school history). He

Mark Thurmond, who was the Game 1 starter in the 1984 World Series, now lives in the Houston area with his wife, Debbie, and his sons, 19-year-old Matt and 17-year-old twins, Drew and Dane. (Photo courtesy of Mark Thurmond)

pitched a no-hitter against Texas Tech in 1978 and compiled a miniscule 2.29 career ERA. But for all the individual accomplishments, Thurmond says his fondest memories of A&M are the championship seasons and the stellar friendships.

"When you look back at what happened with that team, Texas had won the SWC 19 out of 21 years," said Thurmond, whose wife, Debbie, is also an Aggie. "The only two years they did not win it were 1977 and '78 when we won the conference. Those were highlights for me. Looking back, I remember all the great guys and friendships I made. And Coach Chandler was a like a father figure to me. When I came to A&M, I was strung tight as piano wire. Everything was life or death for me on the field. He really helped me enjoy the game more."

Following a disappointing senior season in 1979, when the Aggies failed to make the NCAA playoffs, Thurmond was selected by the Padres in the fifth round. He spent two and a half seasons battling the wind in Amarillo before moving on to AAA ball in Hawaii. A month after the start of the 1983 season, the Padres called him up for a couple of weeks and sent him back down. By that June, however, he was back in the big leagues to stay.

Thurmond's pro career came to an end when he was released by the Giants in July of 1991. He returned home to Houston that summer with thoughts of making another run at baseball the following season. "But the more I sat in my chair at home, the better it felt," he said. "I told myself, 'I've got something I can do here.' I guess I was just ready for the next phase of my life."

Thurmond's father started the Al Thurmond Agency in 1973, specializing in property, casualty, benefits, health, life and disability insurance. Mark's older brother went to work with his father in 1978, and Mark earned his license during his senior year at A&M and worked during every off season while he was in the minor and major leagues.

"My dad and Al would handle things while I was gone, then I'd go to spring training to rest," Mark joked. "The month before spring training was always tough, finishing up here and getting in shape to play for spring training. Going to camp and just working out was a lot easier. But I've always enjoyed this work, and it's been a blessing to me. I've been doing it [since 1980], so I guess I've found my niche."

Thurmond hasn't left baseball completely behind, though. He's still a part-time coach and full-time advisor to his three sons, 19-year-old Matt and 17-year-old twins, Drew and Dane. "I've had a chance to coach them, and that's been fun," Thurmond said. "They have all enjoyed baseball, and it's given us a real bond. I've never wanted to push it on them, but I've tried to share some things along the way."

Perhaps the most important lesson about never giving up can be passed along simply by flipping on Classic Sports and tuning in to that 1984 World Series game. Not bad for a guy who once wondered if he would ever make it out of the windswept Texas Panhandle.

WINSTON
CRITE

During a coaching career that spanned three decades in Aggieland, former Texas A&M football coach R.C. Slocum often proved to have a knack for spotting top talent. And not just gridiron greats. While Slocum was primarily responsible for luring outstanding football players to Texas A&M, the "Silver Fox" also played a hand in landing one of the Aggies' all-time best basketball players.

The tradition of Texas A&M captivated Winston Crite, and Shelby Metcalf closed the deal. But it was Slocum who first spotted Crite as a prospect worth pursuing.

"I never knew Texas A&M existed until R.C. Slocum showed up [in California] one day," said Crite, a native of Bakersfield, California. "R.C. was scouting one of my friends, a guy who played football and basketball. I had pretty much made up my mind that I was going to go to San Diego State. Then the football coaches from A&M walked up to me and were like, 'We've never seen you before.' R.C. said he would go back and tell our basketball coaches about me. The rest is history."

Crite's career at A&M was certainly historic. He broke into the starting lineup as a freshman in 1983-84 and helped lead the Aggies to four consecutive winning seasons, two NIT appearances and a berth in the "Big Dance" during Crite's senior season in 1987. Crite finished his

Photo courtesy of Texas A&M Athletic Media Relations

WINSTON CRITE
A&M Letterman: 1984-87

Sport: Basketball
Position: Forward
First-team All-SWC in 1987
SWC Tournament MVP 1987
All-SWC Defensive Team 1985, '86 and '87
Third-round draft pick of the Phoenix Suns in 1987

career as the third leading scorer in Texas A&M history with 1,576 points. He is also the No. 2 career leader in rebounding with 913 and remains the school's all-time leader in blocked shots with 200.

Of course, numbers tell only part of Crite's charismatic story at A&M. He possessed more "hops" than a beer brewery, energizing the home crowd at G. Rollie White Coliseum with thunderous dunks and fantastic finishes. And perhaps nobody was better in March than Winston Crite. When the games mattered more and the pressure rose, Crite was at his best.

"I think Shelby likes to say I played better at that time of the year, but I don't really think that was the case," Crite said from his office in Bakersfield. "I just think the team required more of me. When it's one game and you're out, the coaches were coming to me saying, 'OK, Winston, give us everything you've got and we're going to get you the ball.' The amount of touches I had went up during that time of the year. They just went to me more."

Crite's finest stretch in an A&M uniform may have come during March 1987. Beginning on March 6, Crite and the Aggies took Dallas's Reunion Arena by storm. A&M entered the Southwest Conference Postseason Tournament as the last-place seed. Coming off a 20-win season in 1985-86, the Aggies started Crite's senior season in strong fashion, compiling a 12-4 overall record and 4-1 mark in SWC play by mid-January. But a road loss to Rice began a miserable slide, as the Aggies lost eight of their final 10 regular-season games. Entering the SWC Tournament, the Aggies weren't even an afterthought.

Against regular-season champion TCU in the opening round of the tournament, however, Metcalf devised a new look. All season long, the Aggies featured a one-man front. But against TCU, A&M came out with a two-man front featuring Todd Holloway and Darryl McDonald. The Aggies' new look spread the floor and opened up the paint for Crite. The high-flying Crite responded by scoring 30 points in an 81-70 win over the "Killer Frogs." Crite was again at his best the next night, as the Aggies upset Texas Tech, 68-60, to earn a spot in the championship game against Baylor.

The Bears managed to slow Crite down somewhat. But Baylor's obsession with Crite opened things up for everybody else in maroon, as the Aggies manhandled Baylor 71-46 to earn a berth in the NCAA Tournament.

"I would say winning the SWC tournament and getting the MVP was probably the highlight of my career at A&M," Crite said. "It was just such a fun run for us. And to be able to finish my college career in the

NCAA Tournament against a team like Duke was a real thrill. My only regret is we didn't knock [Duke] off. We had a chance to get those guys, and then it might have really gotten fun."

Following the Aggies' opening-round loss to Duke in the NCAAs, Crite was selected by Phoenix in the third round of the NBA draft. He played 29 games as a rookie and seemed to have a promising future with the organization. But on a roster that featured stars like Larry Nance and Walter Davis, Crite would soon become a victim of the numbers game and the politics of pro sports. He was released by the Suns early in his second season (1988-89) in the league, ending a dream that had only just begun.

"It was a real dream come true to make it in the NBA," Crite said. "But honestly, it wasn't as fun as college. My first year, I had a sense of, 'goal accomplished.' I got here, which is what I was trying to do all my life. The second year I found out about the political side of the NBA and that it was really about money. They said, 'Winston, you're a great player, but it's not about your skills. This is about the fact that you're making this amount of money and these guys over here are making much more, so we expect a higher return on our investment.' It came down to return on investment. I had to accept that."

After he was released by the Suns, Crite's pro career took wings in Europe. During the next decade, he became a star overseas, with stops in Spain, France, Greece and Italy. Crite left the NBA with a sour taste in his mouth, but his memories of Europe are nothing but sweet.

"In Europe, I grew as a player and a man," Crite said. "I started to enjoy basketball instead of being so intense. I was so intense because I believed at that time that I was one of the best players in the world. That was just my mindset. That's what drove me. But in Europe, I learned to love the game and enjoy the surroundings. I got to the point where Europe was like home. I enjoyed living in Paris, and it became a second home to me."

Crite hung up his high-tops and returned to the United States in 1997. After taking a little time off, he began selling cars in California. In addition to becoming the top salesman for the Mercedes-Benz dealership in his hometown, Crite developed his people skills and became a student of public relations and business in general.

Crite, the father of 14- and 10-year-old boys, says he enjoyed sales, but when an opportunity presented itself in 2003 to get back into the sports world, he jumped at it. Crite is currently the vice president of Recruit, a California-based service that helps high school athletes attract attention from major universities, small colleges, etc. With his basketball background and passion for kids, Crite says he believes he's found his niche.

"Recruit is the leading recruiting service in the U.S.," said Crite, who also runs a membership-based basketball club called "The Footwork Shop" for kids ranging in age from nine to 18. "We help kids get exposure so they can get noticed. My job is to help us create alliances with corporations and to deal with the investors. My role is to continue to help the company grow. It's growing really quickly, and I'm having a blast. The work is stimulating to me. And the Footwork Shop is a lot of fun, too. The Footwork Shop is a yearly basketball clinic I hold here in Bakersfield. It's always been my desire to create a club-like atmosphere where members can develop as players and as people. Our goal is to supplement an athlete's normal coaching at school or on their club team with a unique skills training program that is not available at the high school or college level. And as any coach who knows the game will tell you, the first thing they look at is a player's feet. That's how we came up with the name, 'Footwork Shop.'"

While Crite says it is particularly rewarding to have his own feet planted back home in Bakersfield, he acknowledges that he will always consider College Station his home away from home. Crite recently returned to A&M for a players' reunion and says he will attempt to become more involved with the university he still holds in such high esteem.

"Whether I was in Phoenix, Spain, France, California or wherever else, people always knew I was an Aggie," Crite said. "Being an Aggie is just in you. Once you go to school at A&M, you're an Aggie for life. I'm proud to have gone to school at A&M, and it was a thrill to have played basketball at A&M."

Rest assured, longtime Aggie basketball fans feel the same way. And those A&M fans who watched in delight as Crite won over the hearts of central Texas will always be thankful that R.C. bumped into W.C.

TONY
McGINNIS

From his "office" in Huntsville, Alabama, former Texas A&M guard Tony McGinnis can walk out the back door and see precisely where he grew up. It's not a pleasant stroll down memory lane.

Some changes have been made for the better. But Sparkman Homes, one of the largest public housing developments in Huntsville, is still ravaged with many of the same atrocities McGinnis encountered as a child. As recently as 2001, Census figures showed 84 percent of the households there are headed by women who have an average annual income of $5,752. As McGinnis knows, such poverty attracts crime like ants to a picnic.

"It's a rough neighborhood," says McGinnis, the director of the Sparkman Homes Boys and Girls Club. "It was when I was growing up. It still is. It's considered one of the roughest neighborhoods in Huntsville. People don't come down here because they're afraid. We're talking gunfire, drugs, gangs, loud music and just about anything else you can think of."

McGinnis, who ranks 12th in Texas A&M history with 1,240 career points from 1992-95, doesn't have to be here. He's one of the lucky Sparkman Homes natives—a rare beacon in these parts who chose dreams over drugs. He escaped the neighborhood once, made it to col-

Photo courtesy of Texas A&M Athletic Media Relations

TONY McGINNIS
A&M Letterman: 1992-95

Sport: Basketball
Position: Forward
1994 All-SWC Defensive team
No. 12 scoring leader in A&M history (1,240 points)

lege, thrived in professional basketball overseas and made the most of his opportunities. He could probably still be enjoying celebrity status in Australia, playing the game he loves.

Instead, he's back in the projects he once called home. But please don't feel sorry for him, McGinnis says. He's doing what he was called to do. He might have won fans in Australia, but he's saving lives in Huntsville. McGinnis, a journalism major at A&M, left basketball with no regrets and few second thoughts. In fact, he hung up his high-tops with such grace that he has recently written a book entitled *The Game is Deep*. The book documents the ups and downs of basketball and provides insight into why so many players struggle in life without the sport.

McGinnis obviously isn't one of those people. Basketball was a chapter in his life. But helping others is his life's work. You can see it in the faces of those he works with at the Boys and Girls Club, and you can hear it in his heartfelt words.

"These kids are going through many of the same things I did," McGinnis said. "I have an opportunity to make a difference in their lives. There are some financial things I can't do working here, but the rewards are more than money could ever give me. When I can see a kid who has obstacles in his life make the right decisions, it's everything to me. I thank the Lord I survived that as a child. I was giving my testimony at church, and it's amazing that I was one of the only ones to make it out. So many kids had more talent and were smarter than me. But many of them are in jail or worse. I was blessed to get out—now I want to help some of these kids get out, too."

McGinnis is working miracles, and the kids adore him. He's more than a role model; he's a hero, a friend, a father figure that many of them never had. But while McGinnis relishes his role, he's not satisfied. Reaching at-risk kids early in life is important, but it's not the cure-all. That's why McGinnis is also working toward developing his own mentoring program called "The Diploma Project."

"I've seen so many guys do fine up until they finish eighth grade and reach high school," McGinnis said. "But then that's when they get lost and become involved with the wrong people and things. Through the Diploma Project, I want to branch off and begin mentoring and tracking guys when they are in the fourth or fifth grades and follow them through high school. If I can have that continuing influence, I believe I can have a much more positive long-term impact on them."

If he can save even one of them, his decision to leave basketball behind will be worth it, he says. But then he quickly points out his calling has already produced many wonderful blessings in his life, including a family of his own. After playing one season in Slovenia, McGinnis played for a touring team called Marathon Oil, which plays exhibition games against colleges. He then landed in Australia, where he had a great time and a great season.

He had every intention of returning to Australia the following season. But his life was forever changed when he ended up back at the Sparkman Homes Boys and Girls Club that had been such a positive influence on him as a youth.

"After I left Australia I went back to Texas for a little while and then I came back home, because I thought I was going to get ready to go back to Australia," McGinnis said. "I was planning on just being home for the summer. But God had other plans for me. I went to the Boys and Girls Club, and this beautiful lady was sitting there. She hired me to work that summer. She told me she needed someone who was going to be totally committed to the summer program, and I told her I would definitely be that person. The very next day my agent called me and asked if I was ready to go. He had another offer for me, and I was going to make $10,000 playing in a summer league. It was way more money than I could make working a whole year at the Boys and Girls Club. But I had given my word to this woman. I prayed about that decision, and I knew in my heart that I was supposed to be at the Boys and Girls Club. To make a long story short, God rewarded me for that decision. That beautiful lady and I ended up getting married."

McGinnis has been married to Kreslyn since March of 1999. The couple's first child together, Antonio Leon McGinnis, Jr., was born on April 24, 2001. They also have two older children (ages 12 and 10) McGinnis has adopted.

McGinnis is a spokesman for the power of prayer. And his stories regarding how his prayers have been answered have a way of reaching the kids he works with. One such story still causes chills to run up McGinnis's spine, and it still brings Dave South, A&M's associate athletic director/sponsorships and broadcasts, to the brink of tears. As a freshman in 1991, McGinnis was down in the dumps when he went down to his knees. The answer he received still amazes him.

"[Former A&M coach Tony] Barone just went crazy on me," McGinnis said. "He was trying to see who was tough enough to cut it. But it went on for days and weeks, and I got so beaten down. I was thinking I couldn't take it any more. I was in my room at Cain Hall praying. I was crying and thinking I was just going to go home and get a regular job. But I prayed for God to send somebody into my life to give me

Tony McGinnis has been married to Kreslyn since March of 1999 and adopted her two children. The couple's first child together, Antonio Leon McGinnis Jr., was born on April 24, 2001. (Photo courtesy of Tony McGinnis)

a little comfort. I was so specific that I prayed for God to send somebody into my room that night if it was meant for me to stay at Texas A&M."

Almost immediately, McGinnis's academic advisor knocked on his door. McGinnis was impressed, but not yet convinced.

"I thought that was a coincidence, because he was going to come by anyway," he said. "I was still doubting, so I started praying again, asking God to send me a real sign. Well, then Dave South comes to my room, knocks on the door and says, 'Tony, I was just thinking about you. Keep your head up, son. You're going to make it.' He had never been to my room before. Not once. I said. 'God, I believe it now. I'm staying.'"

Fortunately for the Aggies, he did more than merely stay. McGinnis had solid freshman and sophomore seasons and then helped lead the Aggies to a 19-11 record and an NIT berth as a junior in 1993-94. He averaged 10.0 points as a junior and 15.2 as a senior. He also led the Aggies in blocked shots as a junior and steals as a senior.

"You always look back and wish things could have been a little better," McGinnis said of his time at A&M. "But things were pretty good my last two seasons. We went to the NIT and had a chance to win the conference that year. Plus, I played with some guys who I will never forget and played in front of some crowds I'll never forget. I still have plenty of maroon pride in me. I stand up for the Aggies here in Alabama. I'll see guys from time to time with A&M stickers on their car or wearing T-shirts, and I always tell them how much I loved my time at Texas A&M. Being at A&M helped shape my life, and I'm a better man because of it."

A&M also is a better place because of Tony McGinnis—what he did while in College Station and how he continues to represent the university.

TREY MOORE

Growing up, Warren Moore III—better known as Trey—never spent too much time fantasizing about being a baseball celebrity. But when the idea occasionally crossed his mind, Moore figured that—if he ever achieved such a status—he would enjoy every minute of it.

He was wrong. In Japan, Moore has reached a level of international popularity that he would have once never even dreamed possible. While he most often relishes the spotlight, Moore admits there are times when he simply wishes he could blend into the crowd. Moore has become so popular in Japan that in 2003 he resorted to purchasing and wearing an Elvis Presley wig so that he would not be harassed by fans while out in public with his family.

"Baseball is by far the most popular sport in Japan," said Moore, a starting pitcher for the Aggies from 1992-94. "It got to a point where I couldn't go anywhere in my home city without being recognized or causing a scene. You always have people who will stare at you, and that's fine. But you also have the loud fans who are yelling and pointing at me. It's a situation that you almost dream about in terms of being a superstar. It's hard to complain about that. But it is bad when you are with your family, and I can't stand in a line without having 20 people coming up to me to take pictures. I have a shaved head and a mustache, and there aren't

Photo courtesy of Texas A&M Athletic Media Relations

TREY MOORE
A&M Letterman: 1992-94

Sport: Baseball
Position: Pitcher
First-team All-SWC pitcher in 1993
Second-round draft pick of Seattle Mariners in 1994
Japanese All-Star Game 2002

many people walking around the streets of Japan that look like me. I stick out in a crowd. So I bought the wig, but I still got plenty of stares, probably because I looked so goofy. If I would have had a robe on they would have thought I was a monk."

Nevertheless, Moore is generally elated to be dealing with such inconveniences. Not so long ago, Moore seemed to be in the twilight of his baseball career. Now he's shining brightly in the Land of the Rising Sun.

Moore debuted in the major leagues in 1998 with Montreal, resurfaced in the bigs in 2000 after undergoing shoulder surgery and appeared briefly with the Atlanta Braves in 2001. His career major league totals— 23 games, 100.3 innings worked and a 5.83 ERA—were not going to earn any calls from Cooperstown.

But to Moore, they did signify he had answered his life's calling. From the time he could remember, all Moore ever really wanted to do was play baseball at Texas A&M. He did that and then some, leading the Aggies to the 1993 College World Series, working his way through the minor leagues and making it to baseball's ultimate high-rent district.

So as the 2001 season ended, Moore, then 28, knew that if this was the end of his baseball road, he could walk away from the game with two satisfying words: Mission accomplished. But just when it appeared as if Moore might be relegated back to the minor leagues or released altogether, Japan came calling—on December 7, 2001, of all days—as the Hanshin Tigers of the Japanese Central League purchased Moore's rights from the Braves.

The decision to leave the United States for Japan was the easiest no-brainer for Moore since the lifelong Aggie fan chose Texas A&M as his collegiate destination. In Japan, Moore would have the opportunity to make more money in one season than if he stuck around for two or three more years in the major leagues.

With a fresh start in a new country, Moore has been magnificent. He was an All-Star in his first season with the Tigers and started Game 7 of the Japan World Series in 2003, compiling a 10-6 record despite an injury-hampered regular season. In 2004, he joined the Orix Blue Wave of the Pacific League. The team was so excited for Moore to be on the roster that the marketing department pasted the left-hander's mug on jackets and windbreakers prior to the start of the season and sold replica Moore mustaches to the fans.

And despite some occasional headaches with the fans, Moore is enjoying his role as an "American Idol" in Japan. But playing the American pastime in the Pacific Rim has created awkward adjustments and inconveniences for Moore and his family. For example, Moore had to train himself not to spit on the ground during games because the Japanese view the field as sacred. Then there's the language barrier. Moore has picked up bits and pieces of the language over time, but he's firmly convinced he'll never master the printed word.

"No chance," he said with a laugh. "There are about 8,000 characters in the alphabet. I can understand more words than I can speak. I can pick up a few words and put together what they are asking me. I always have my translator there with me when I'm talking to the media. But when we first got over there, it was really difficult, and we didn't want to leave the little area where our apartment is. We didn't want to venture too far because we were afraid we couldn't ask how to get back. The other thing that was really difficult was learning the trains. Once you can learn your route and not veer too far off of it, you're fine. But you can get lost. It was hard, but my wife got real comfortable and she has the trains down now."

Moore and his wife, Tia, have two children, 11-year-old Warren Moore IV, who goes by "Ford," and eight-year-old Abigail. The Moores own a home in College Station, and both of the kids attend College Station schools. But Tia and the kids join Moore in Japan after spring break, where the kids finish out the school year at the Canadian Academy, which features an international, English-speaking school not far from where the Moores reside on Roko Island.

"They both have friends there through the academy, and they look forward to going back to see those friends," he said. "The curriculum is a little different and is more hands-on, but I think it balances out well. They do a field trip every other week and go to the castles and to the beaches to dig for clams. One hour a day, they also take Japanese classes, so they are really learning things they would never learn in the U.S. Then in the first week of August, my wife and kids will come back here and get ready to start school. I'm lucky enough to have married a very strong woman who can take on the role of single parent for half of the year when I leave. And I remind my kids that there is going to be a time when I am going to be here all the time, and I will be staying on top of them. One day, they might be wishing I was gone. But right now, we're all having fun. I'm not ready to stop playing any time soon. Besides, I am not ready for those Texas summers yet."

Perhaps not, but the heat of Olsen Field brings to mind plenty of great memories for Moore. He grew up in Keller dreaming of wearing the maroon and white, as both his father and his grandfather were A&M graduates. Once he arrived in College Station, Moore was a key contrib-

Trey Moore and his wife, Tia, have two children, 11-year-old Warren Moore IV and eight-year-old Abigail. The Moores own a home in College Station. Tia and the kids join Moore in Japan, where he pitches for the Orix Blue Wave, after spring break, where the kids finish out the school year at the Canadian Academy. (**Photo courtesy of Trey Moore**)

utor to the pitching staff as a freshman and then began dominating opponents as a sophomore. Joining Jeff Granger at the top of the weekend pitching rotation, Moore went 12-0 in 1993 with a 2.77 ERA as the Aggies advanced to Omaha. Moore also hit .314 as a sophomore with 24 RBI and four homers.

But of all the individual accomplishments and big wins, Moore still says his favorite memory of his playing days at Texas A&M was probably the first time he ever slipped on the Aggies' uniform.

"I was groomed to be an Aggie, so putting on that uniform was a big deal to me," said Moore, who compiled a three-year record of 19-7. "So when I got that scholarship offer, it was quite a big deal for me and my father. That was the fulfillment of all the work we had put in together. I'll never forget the run we had to the World Series, but seeing 'Aggies' across my own uniform for the first time was the biggest dream come true for me."

Dreams continued to come true for Moore when the Seattle Mariners selected him in the second round of the 1994 amateur draft. Moore was dealt to the Expos' organization in 1996 and appeared in his first major league game in 1998 with Montreal. At that point, it seemed as if Moore might be headed for international acclaim. And he was, of course. But it took a little longer than expected and required several unique detours, as he went from north of the border to the Deep South and then finally to the Far East.

"It's been an interesting ride," Moore acknowledged. "And I'm certainly grateful for the opportunity that opened up in Japan. It's really worked out well."

It's worked out exceptionally well, and when he's not forced into costume, he's enjoying every minute of it.

STACY SYKORA

Prior to the 2000 Olympic Games in Sydney, Australia, Stacy Denise Sykora gleefully predicted that she would participate in at least four or five Olympics and might want to still be competing until she was 40. But as she prepared for the 2004 Games in Athens, Greece, Sykora was suddenly singing a different tune.

The 2004 Games, she said, would probably be her last. Playing volleyball year-round for so long had begun to take its toll on her. Besides, the self-proclaimed flower-power chick is no longer such a spring chicken. She was 27 when the 2004 Games began and—perish the thought—closing in on the big "three-oh," which once seemed as archaic to her as Athens.

"I'm getting on up there," said the free-spirited Sykora, who in 2000 became the first Aggie ever to participate in Olympic volleyball. "But don't for one minute think I'm getting all mature. I'm still me, and I'm still as wacky as ever. I don't think I have changed much. I'm still out there."

Out there, indeed. As in out there on another wavelength, another dimension or another planet. You may not find it in astronomy or cosmology textbooks, but trust us. "Stacy's World" is still there and is just as fascinating and flamboyant as ever. You can enter her world for a fast-

Photo courtesy of Texas A&M Media Relations

STACY SYKORA
A&M Letterman: 1995-98

Sport: Volleyball
Position: Outside Hitter
Two-time AVCA All-American outside hitter
Three-sport letterman at A&M
Starting libero on the 2000 USA Olympic team

paced, fun-filled visit, but extended stays are not advised. Most earth-dwelling mortals simply do not possess the perpetual energy or nonstop outlandishness to stay orbiting with the cosmic adventures of Sykora, who sports a pierced tongue, a pierced nose and a pierced chin to go along with her piercing blue eyes.

Sykora, who played at A&M from 1995-98 and also lettered in basketball and track, is quite possibly the greatest player in Aggie volleyball history. She may also be the best female athlete in A&M history. While that is up for debate, there's no denying that Sykora is one of the most unforgettably unique personalities in the university's history.

When she last resided in Aggieland, Sykora earned a well-deserved reputation for being as colorful as the Crayola assembly line. Her teammates often joked that they could make a comfortable living simply by charging admission to see Sykora's room, which was as eccentric as her personality.

Among various other things, her sensory-overloaded living quarters featured love beads, a disco ball, Christmas lights, flowery Sykora paintings, a jumbo portrait of a Volkswagen "Magic Bus," assorted butterflies and frogs, incense, a glowing pink telephone and a remarkably large poster of former Chicago Bulls bad boy Dennis Rodman (her all-time favorite sports hero). She's a child of the '60s who happened to be born in the late '70s, combining the shock value of Ozzy Osborne on stage with the flair of Liberace and the zaniness of Robin Williams.

But for all of her peculiar personality traits and preferences, what truly distinguished Sykora during her A&M days was the way she performed on the volleyball court. The two-time All-American outside hitter could leap out of the building and regularly brought the crowd at G. Rollie White to its feet with her explosive kills. On the floor, she combined the grace of a ballet dancer with the showmanship of a pro wrestler.

"She was definitely one of a kind on and off the floor," said A&M volleyball coach Laurie Corbelli, a member of the 1984 USA Olympic team. "She's the most incredible athlete I've ever coached and maybe even the most incredible athlete I've been in the gym with. I've been in the gym with some amazing athletes, but especially from a defensive standpoint, her speed and lightning quickness make her sensational. I don't think any of us realized what she provided the program, but it still perpetuates. I credit her for teaching the team to have a good time when they played and to kind of see the lighter side of competition, although she may be one of the most serious competitors I've ever met. But she had a way of teaching the team and staff to lighten up. I still remember times that I did not want to laugh when she pointed at her biceps and called them her guns and kissed them after a kill. I didn't want to laugh, but I couldn't help it. She's always stood out from the crowd."

She still does. Sykora remains the queen of self-expression, tantalizing fans and thriving in the spotlight of the crowd. But to her delight, Sykora's stage evolved from regional to international. She first took her high-flying, high-voltage act to the 2000 Olympics and, as the squad's libero (defensive specialist), helped Team USA to an impressive finish that placed the Americans just short of the bronze medal. She was one of the darlings of the U.S. team and was certainly one of the most photogenic.

Even after the Games, the toned, defined and eye-catching Sykora appeared in a 2002 *Sports Illustrated* photo shoot with numerous other athletes from various sports in nothing but her undergarments. Sykora says she wasn't crazy about the picture, and she scoffs at the notion that she is now a sex symbol. But there's no doubt that the inclusion of her sleek physique in *SI* added to her national prominence, and her performance overseas gave her international acclaim. Following the 2000 Games, Sykora signed to play professional volleyball in Italy, where the sport is extremely popular.

It didn't take long for the entertaining and attractive Sykora to become one of the league's more popular stars. Italian fans fell in love with her skills, hustle and showmanship. Likewise, Sykora fell for Italy's culture, history and lifestyle. The salary opportunities for professional volleyball players were also quite appealing.

"I've really enjoyed playing in Italy," Sykora said. "I like the language; I like learning the culture. The food, the people, the lifestyle are all completely different from what I knew growing up in Burleson or going to school at A&M. I like different things sometimes, and I like to have change. Plus, volleyball is really big in Italy. It is the biggest women's sport they have. My first year was a shock because everything is so different. That year was tough, but it was a good experience, and I wanted to go back because I really fell in love with it. I have been going back every year since because I really like it. And the pay is wonderful in Italy. You can't make any money playing pro volleyball in the United States, but you can make six figures easily in Italy."

While Sykora has made a nice living overseas and made an even bigger impact on the Italian fans, she maintained her ties to USA Volleyball. She continually played for the U.S. national team during her summers and falls, and after the 2004 professional season ended, she

In 2000, Stacy Sykora became the first Aggie ever to participate in Olympic volleyball. Sykora has also been an international star in professional volleyball. (Photo courtesy of USA Volleyball)

returned to the U.S. to focus on making the U.S. Olympic team one more time.

"I dreamed about the Olympics ever since I was small and would always talk about the Olympics," she said prior to the 2004 Games. "To actually be out there during opening ceremonies, which is something you can't even describe, was incredible. Then actually playing in the Olympics was awesome. But after the '04 Games, I am going to take a break, re-evaluate my life and see where I am going with it."

For someone with Sykora's personality, style and flair, the possibilities seem endless. While nothing is set in stone, Sykora says show business does have a certain appeal. She's given some thought to becoming a volleyball coach, but she is leaning more toward giving acting a shot. And if that dream comes to fruition, she may reclaim her unofficial title as Burleson's most famous female. She probably held that title until Kelly Clarkson won the *American Idol* competition in 2002, thrusting her into the national spotlight. While Sykora loves being the center of attention in any setting, she acknowledges that Clarkson may now have more national name recognition. But don't think for one minute that Sykora is content with playing second fiddle to anyone, especially someone from her hometown.

"Right now, I'd probably have to give the nod to Kelly Clarkson because she is more nationally known," Sykora said. "But I would have to take the international level honor myself. I think I am more internationally known. And if I become an actress and get into movies, look out world."

No matter what route Sykora chooses, Corbelli is confident she will be a success. Along with being outrageous, Sykora possesses an amazing resolve that continually drives her toward success. And despite what Sykora might want you to believe, she is even displaying quite a bit of maturity as she nears 30.

"Stacy has realized a lot of things about life since she left A&M," Corbelli said. "She has apologized to me for her rebelliousness in one of her years, in particular. To me, that shows a lot of maturity. I think she has matured a whole bunch, but the core personality to Stacy is still the carefree, live-for-each-day type that we all knew and loved. She still loves to make people laugh, and I hope that never changes. She may not like the word 'maturity,' but she is growing up and growing better. I'm really proud of not only what she's done, but also what she's becoming."

Celebrate the Heroes of College Football

in These Other 2004 Releases from Sports Publishing

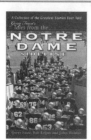

Gerry Faust's Tales from the Notre Dame Sideline
by Gerry Faust, John Heisler, and Bob Logan

- 5.5 x 8.25 hardcover
- 200 pages
- photos throughout
- $19.95

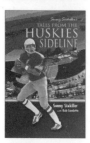

Sonny Sixkiller's Tales from the Huskies Sideline
by Sonny Sixkiller
with Bob Condotta

- 5.5 x 8.25 hardcover
- 200 pages
- vintage photos throughout
- $19.95

Tales from the Boston College Sideline
by Reid Oslin

- 5.5 x 8.25 hardcover
- 200+ pages
- photos throughout
- $19.95

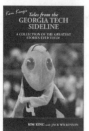

Kim King's Tales from the Georgia Tech Sideline
by Kim King
with Jack Wilkinson

- 5.5 x 8.25 hardcover
- 200 pages
- photos throughout
- $19.95

Tales from the Miami Hurricanes Sideline
by Jim Martz

- 5.5 x 8.25 hardcover
- 200 pages
- photos throughout
- $19.95

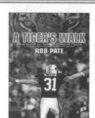

A Tiger's Walk: Memoirs of an Auburn Football Player
by Rob Pate

- 6 x 9 hardcover • 250 pages
- 8-page color-photo section
- $24.95

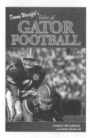

Danny Wuerffel's Tales of Florida Football
by Danny Wuerffel
with Mike Bianchi

- 5.5 x 8.25 hardcover
- 200 pages
- photos throughout
- $19.95

Legends of Alabama Football
by Richard Scott

- 8.5 x 11 hardcover
- 200+ pages
- photos throughout
- $19.95

Michigan: Where Have You Gone?
by Jim Cnockaert

- 6 x 9 hardcover
- 250+ pages
- 50+ photos throughout
- $24.95

Saturdays: Between the Hedges
by Jeff Dantzler
Photography by Radi Nabul

- 9 x 12 hardcover
- 160 pages
- 200 color photos througho
- $29.95

To order at any time, please call toll-free **877-424-BOOK (2665)**.
For fast service and quick delivery, order on-line at **www.SportsPublishingLLC.com**.